TRUMPEDIA

TRUMPEDIA

Alternative facts about a real fake president

Dominic Knight

ALLEN&UNWIN
SYDNEY•MELBOURNE•AUCKLAND•LONDON

First published in 2018

Allen & Unwin
83 Alexander Street
Crows Nest NSW 2065
Australia
Phone: (61 2) 8425 0100
Email: info@allenandunwin.com
Web: www.allenandunwin.com

 A catalogue record for this
book is available from the
National Library of Australia

ISBN 978 1 76052 736 5

Set in 10/18 pt Helvetica Neue by Bookhouse, Sydney

10 9 8 7 6 5 4 3 2 1

For Indira,
*with apologies for bringing you
into a world run by this guy*

Legal disclaimer

This book is fake news. Its author never wrote a *New York Times* bestseller like *The Art Of The Deal* by Donald J. Trump. Sad!

While the book contains entries about well-known subjects and people, none of the 'facts' cited should be taken as true in any way whatsoever, as the author is a member of the lying, failing media, who are so dishonest, especially about President Trump.

Each entry in this book is based on the corresponding Wikipedia entry — indeed, few other sources have been used, because we live in a post-truth society and it doesn't matter whether anything in this book is accurate. Just go with your gut, like so many of us do when a 'scientist' claims that a 'fact' is 'proven', or when a billionaire who has never done anything in his life that wasn't for himself promises that he's the only one who can save our low-paid job and hardscrabble town.

Reading any page of this book creates attorney–client privilege between you and the author, and also binds the reader in a non-disclosure agreement that prevents you ('Peggy Peterson') from taking any legal action against the author ('David Dennison') or publisher ('Thomas Thompson') for anything, ever.

A portion of the proceeds from this book will be donated to the Wikimedia Foundation to help make Wikipedia great again. The author contends that Wikipedia is the most remarkable thing ever to happen on the internet besides the 2016 US presidential election.

Note to readers

In the interests of improving the mix of entries for the reader, their order has been alphabetised as though the word 'Trump' were removed, as it has been from so many buildings since the election. The result is that most of the members of the Trump family are not found next to one another, which should reduce their opportunities for collusion.

All figures are in US Dollars, the currency in which Donald J. Trump is supposedly a billionaire.

The author is on Twitter, the world's leading social network for pointless, angry disputes. Readers can start a frustrating, futile argument with him by tweeting @domknight.

Access Hollywood

Access Hollywood is the television program on which Donald Trump made a guest appearance when he was recorded boasting of his penchant for sexual assault, and how when you're a star, women let you do it. The show's host, Billy Bush, was fired for his apparent encouragement of Trump's behaviour and, due to the scandal, became the only male member of the Bush family who has not run for president—yet.

For his part, Trump learned that the other thing they let you do when you're a star is rapidly put a huge scandal behind you, and go on to grab the presidency as well.

America First

To the extent to which Donald Trump has an internally consistent foreign policy, it can be summarised via the slogan **America First**.

Trump maintains that the country boasting the world's strongest and wealthiest economy, and unchallenged military might, is nevertheless treated unfairly by the rest of the world. It must therefore renegotiate its relationships even with its closest allies like Canada, with its irritatingly attractive prime minister, and the EU, with its irritatingly German Angela Merkel.

History of the term

Like 'Make America Great Again', 'America First' is a phrase with a long history in American politics, to which Trump is oblivious. In the early nineteenth century, white-hooded Klansmen and women marched with banners demanding 'America First', and the phrase is still used by KKK Grand Wizard and Trump supporter David Duke.

In his 1916 re-election campaign, Woodrow Wilson used the isolationist slogan 'He kept us out of War. America First.' After winning re-election, Wilson ordered American troops to fight anyway, and went on to found the League of Nations, meaning that he ultimately made 'America First' his lowest priority.

The slogan was adopted by former Nixon staffer and far-right ideologue Pat Buchanan when he ran for president three times during the 1990s. His rants against unfair treatment from trading partners like Japan, and warnings about white America being swamped by Hispanics, presaged Trump's own campaign, meaning that Buchanan used 'America First' first.

Most recently, Trump used the phrase in his inaugural address, saying that 'from this moment on, it's going to be America First'. In just the first half of his first term, Trump has already had more success than any of his rhetorical predecessors in delivering on the 'America First' vision of a more blinkered and selfish America.

Meaning under Trump

Donald Trump's approach to politics is transactional—for him 'America First' involves treating America as an extension of himself, and consequently demanding special treatment. Just as Trump demands tax concessions from local authorities on all of his construction projects, he also believes that the 'very unfair' norms of the global order need not apply to the country he runs.

Whether the subject is a trade deal, a US base overseas, or even America's Cold War-winning leadership of NATO, previous standards no longer apply. For Trump, it's weak and foolish for America to take any action just because it seems right or benevolent. But once he's on board, his praise will be lavish, no matter how desperate and starving his new friend's citizenry may be, or how many uncles he might have killed with anti-aircraft guns.

Policy implications

Some of the policy changes deriving from Trump's America First stance, and their effects, are as follows:

- **reconsider NAFTA**—antagonise America's neighbours and major customers
- **impose a travel ban**—antagonise Muslims, and boost terrorist recruitment
- **pull America out of the Trans-Pacific Partnership**—encourage allies to club together without America
- **impose tariffs in key industries and for major trading partners**—start a trade war that devastates many American businesses
- **threaten to pull out of America's overseas bases**—establish a protection racket
- **pull out of the Paris climate accord**—cut off America's nose to spite its face, then not be able to breathe clean air through the hole where its nose once was
- **pull America out of the Iran deal**—replace a deal discouraging Iran from developing nuclear weapons with no disincentive whatsoever

- **taunt and threaten North Korea**—play chicken with a nuclear power led by an inexperienced, erratic, unpredictable leader, who will nevertheless outnegotiate Trump when they sit down for a summit
- **recognise Jerusalem as Israel's capital**—put the pet issue of major Republican donors in America First

Family exception

America First is the political equivalent of the rule by which Trump has always conducted his business: 'Family First'. This earlier principle overrides America First where there is conflict between the two objectives, such as when the Trump Organization or Kushner Companies has a business deal involving state parties.

For instance, government ethics experts* have expressed concern about the link between a Chinese government-owned company helping finance a Trump hotel and golf project in Indonesia, and the president's abrupt about-face on his sanctions against the Chinese smartphone company ZTE, about which he tweeted 'Too many jobs

America First, and White Americans Firster.

---

* Don Fox, former general counsel of the United States Office of Government Ethics, told Associated Press that the Chinese 'knew exactly what they were investing in', and that this most likely influenced Trump's ZTE comments. Many commentators found his support for ZTE unusual, not just because it was a Chinese company, but because the only tech company he previously seemed to care about was Twitter.

in China lost', displaying a hitherto unseen concern for a competitor's employment market.

Also, Trump's Family First priority does not apply to his sexual partners, as consecutive spouses have found to their surprise and disappointment.

 Donald J. Trump
@realDonaldTrump

It's not a Muslim ban! Not after the White House Counsel said I couldn't call it that! Plus some of our best Customers at Trump Washington DC are from Qatar and Saudi Arabia. The ones I want to keep out of our beautiful Country most are the lying, failing media!

The Apprentice

The Apprentice was a reality television show in which contestants vied for celebrity and wealth, while avoiding victory in the overall competition so as not to waste a year of their lives working for Donald Trump.

The only venture of Trump's career to engage a majority of the American population, *The Apprentice* rated spectacularly well despite being a lengthy infomercial for the Trump Organization's underwhelming products and services.

At the climax of each episode, the losing team faced Trump and his advisers in the 'boardroom', where he would select a contestant to be eliminated with the catchphrase 'You're fired.' This soon became an iconic pop culture phrase and known as the quote most associated with Trump himself, replacing 'We're bankrupt.'

Origins

When Donald Trump was first approached by reality television legend Mark Burnett about appearing in a new show, he was reluctant—he told friends that reality television was 'for the bottom-feeders of society'*. But after being reminded he had run casinos in Atlantic City, Trump realised it was a perfect fit.

Belatedly, it dawned on Trump that not only would he be paid to host and co-produce the program, but that the tasks he assigned could promote his businesses on prime-time television. But even this intensive publicity wasn't enough to make a success of Trump's casino, steak, necktie or vodka enterprises. If only he could have sought advice from someone who knew how to run a successful conglomerate—a business guru who could have taken Trump on as an apprentice.

As the seasons progressed, Ivanka began starring in many of the climactic boardroom scenes, winning fans and providing a platform to launch her own branded goods. Eric and Donald Junior were also tolerated occasionally.

The Celebrity Apprentice

When the format began to grow stale, Burnett and Trump decided to launch a celebrity version—*The Celebrity Apprentice*—which revived interest in the series. This edition ultimately filmed more seasons than the original, as each season introduced new contestants more successful and widely liked than Donald Trump himself.

---

* According to Marc Fisher's 2016 *Washington Post* article, Trump also insisted that his jet appear in every episode, and planned to pitch a *West Wing*-style show about real estate development called *The Tower*. In the pilot script, the hero is called John Barron.

Donald and Ivanka on set with their apprentice. *(Douglas Gorenstein/NBC)*

The New Celebrity Apprentice

After Trump launched his presidential campaign with a fusillade of racist comments, NBC fired him and rebooted the series as *The New Celebrity Apprentice,* hosted by movie star and former California governor Arnold Schwarzenegger. Arnie replaced Trump's 'You're fired' with his own catchphrase—'You're terminated'—because as a business mentor, he deemed it best to remind his protégés of his role as a terrifying killer robot from the future.

However, Trump couldn't resist repeatedly mocking Schwarzenegger—who'd criticised his divisive campaign—for his lower ratings, even though Trump was supposedly busy being president at the time, and also one of the show's executive producers and therefore literally invested in its success. But Trump's scornful tweets backfired, as they provided

Schwarzenegger with an excuse for the reboot's poor ratings, and a reason to resign after one season. What's more, although his time as a host had been relatively unsuccessful, Schwarzenegger is not only a bigger name in the entertainment industry, but was far more effective at governing.

Among the more notable contestants to participate in the show's celebrity version were:

- **Piers Morgan**—The British tabloid-editor-turned-talk-show-host won the first season by being as aggressive and generally unpleasant as Trump himself, all too easy for Morgan.
- **Stephen Baldwin**—Although one Baldwin brother impersonates Trump on *SNL*, this lesser Baldwin is a die-hard supporter of the president, while their brother Billy has accused Trump of hitting on his wife. It's a complicated family. Baldwin made a Christian skateboarding DVD called *Livin' It*, which contains what he terms a 'real message about life'. Apparently, he has distributed in excess of 100,000.
- **Nadia Comăneci**—The gymnast who famously scored a perfect ten from the judges at the Montreal Olympics somehow found herself being judged by a slob with a comb-over.
- **Vincent Pastore**—Famous for his *Sopranos* role as Salvatore 'Big Pussy' Bonpensiero, Pastore was lucky to get through *The Celebrity Apprentice* without being grabbed by the future president.
- **Tito Ortiz**—The mixed martial arts legend had no chance of victory given his Mexican ancestry, and was deported from Trump Tower in week nine.
- **Omarosa Manigault-Newman**—Despite being fired in no fewer than three seasons of *The Apprentice*, she would later be shocked to find working in Trump's White House less than enjoyable.
- **Joan Rivers**—Rivers won season two of *The Celebrity Apprentice* thanks to deploying comic insults that were even better than Trump's.

- **Khloé Kardashian**—The mandatory reality series Kardashian.
- **Rod Blagojevich**—This former Illinois governor was impeached and removed from office for corruption, but welcomed onto a top-rating television program nevertheless. Trump may soon ask him for tips.
- **Sharon Osbourne**—Sharon was initially the hot favourite for season three thanks to her experience with handling older men in the early stages of dementia.
- **La Toya Jackson**—The available Jackson.
- **David Cassidy**—Also available.
- **Meat Loaf**—Trump was always going to invite the man named after his favourite dish to appear on his show.
- **Debbie Gibson**—The 1980s teen pop star has spent most of this millennium appearing on reality shows. In terms of prominence, her *Apprentice* appearance ranks below *Dancing With The Stars*, but above *Skating With Celebrities*.
- **Arsenio Hall**—Hall won season five, a rare instance of an African-American emerging a victor from any process managed by Donald Trump. After this successful return to television, *The Arsenio Hall Show* was re-commissioned, then re-cancelled, leading many to think it might have been kinder if he'd remained in involuntary retirement.
- **Trace Adkins**—The winner of season six, which was populated by contestants from previous seasons because there were no remaining celebrities in America willing to appear on *The Celebrity Apprentice*.
- **Leeza Gibbons**—Whoever she is, she won season seven, Trump's final season as host.
- **Boy George**, **Carson Kressley** from the original *Queer Eye*, **Jon Lovitz** from *SNL*, **Vince Neil** from Mötley Crüe and **Nicole 'Snooki' Polizzi** from *Jersey Shore* were the least obscure stars to appear on *The New Celebrity Apprentice*, collective proof that the poor ratings for season eight were hardly Arnold Schwarzenegger's fault.

Donald J. Trump
@realDonaldTrump

Arnold Schwarzenegger is a joke! He was worse at hosting the show than I was and he won't do so well at undermining the next host either.

Donald J. Trump Presents The Ultimate Merger

This spin-off series from 2010 featured one of the most famous *Apprentice* contestants, Omarosa Manigault-Newman, who had been portrayed as a villain in the original *Apprentice* and *The Celebrity Apprentice*. Over eight episodes, twelve contestants competed for Omarosa's affections, following the unlikely premise that anybody would take relationship advice from Donald Trump. At the end of the season, Omarosa was left with a 'winner', who was then also eliminated because he was still legally married. Consequently, there was no merger, let alone an ultimate one.

Legacy

Trump's time on *The Apprentice* was key to the successful reinvention of his public image after a period of severe financial difficulty in the 1990s. Trump's persona from the show—tough, decisive, straight-talking, with impeccable business judgement and a huge pile of assets—formed the image that he successfully exploited in his campaign, even though it was largely fictitious.

The reports of Trump's sexist behaviour on set—frequent comments about female contestants' breast size and demeaning speculation about which of them he wanted to have sex with—are also very much in keeping with Trump's public persona. He has been accused of sexual assault by former

Apprentice contestant Summer Zervos. Trump denies any wrongdoing, as he does regarding the claims of eighteen other women who have so far come forward—but via these #MeToo accusations, despite changing careers, Trump still has much in common with some of the best-known entertainers and media executives in the world.

The Art of the Deal

Trump: The Art of the Deal* is itself the best deal Trump ever made. It topped the *New York Times* bestseller list for thirteen weeks, has sold more than a million copies, and Trump didn't even have to write a word.

Trump's 'co-writer'—more correctly, the author, Tony Schwartz—assembled it by interviewing Trump, and then, when his subject got bored with the process (after a few minutes), listened in to his calls (with Trump's consent) and cobbled the fragments of Trumpspeak he heard into a coherent narrative. Schwartz says if he wrote the book today, it would be called *The Sociopath*.

The book concerns Trump's childhood in Queens, his first projects in Brooklyn and his early work in Manhattan. Perhaps the most famous part of the book is Trump's statement that he uses 'truthful hyperbole', which is 'an innocent form of exaggeration—and . . . a very effective form of promotion'. He takes the same approach to politics, except nowadays his hyperbole isn't truthful.

---

* Though commonly known as *The Art of the Deal*, the book's formal title has Trump's name in it, presumably so that the word 'TRUMP' could appear in huge letters on the cover, just in case the byline and photo weren't clear enough.

Trump says that *The Art of the Deal* is his second-favourite book after the Bible, although it's not clear that he has read either.

Baby Trump blimp

A **blimp** portraying Donald Trump as a six-metre-high baby, with a scowl and a mobile phone clutched in his tiny hands, was flown in London's Parliament Square during Trump's first visit to the city as president in July 2018. Tens of thousands of protesters attended, though the Trump White House—for the first time ever—sought to downplay crowd numbers.

The blimp was authorised by London's mayor, Sadiq Khan, whom Trump has criticised on multiple occasions, because, as Trump is learning with tariffs, what goes around comes around.

The blimp is not to scale—Trump's actual hands are far smaller. *(Michael Reeve)*

Trump reacted negatively to the blimp, saying 'I guess when they put out blimps to make me feel unwelcome, no reason for me to go to London.' As a result, dozens of other cities have asked the artist Matt Bonner if they can purchase a Trump blimp of their own to guard against future visits. New York City Council has asked about installing a permanent flotilla outside Trump Tower.

Alec Baldwin

Alexander Rae Baldwin III is a writer, producer, comedian and actor. He is the eldest Baldwin brother, and well known for an extensive career in both film and television. He has won three Primetime Emmy Awards, three more than Donald Trump, although it must be noted that the most recent Emmy was for playing Donald Trump.

 Donald J. Trump
@realDonaldTrump

Baldwin is copying the original Donald Trump character developed by me over decades, and uses Trump-authored expressions like Sad™, Fake News™, Ghina™, Ivanka™ and Putin™. These are trademarks of the Trump Organization and related entities such as the Ivanka Trump Collection and the Russian government. I will sue!

Steve Bannon

White House chief strategist and senior counsellor to the president, 20 January 2017–18 August 2018

Stephen Kevin Mephistopheles Bannon has been a media executive, political adviser, investment banker, movie producer, naval officer, de facto president of the United States, and would-be puppetmaster of America's transformation into a white nationalist oligarchic hellscape modelled on the movie *Mad Max Beyond Thunderdome*.

Bannon was Donald Trump's final campaign manager, and became his chief strategist in the White House. Tensions arose, however, when Bannon was portrayed by the source Trump believes is the planet's most authoritative signifier of status, *Time* magazine, as 'The Great Manipulator', because he was the only person in the Trump administration with any concrete policy ideas. (The term 'concrete' is apt because the adoption of these ideas immediately caused Trump's approval ratings to sink to the bottom of the Potomac River.)

For a time, Bannon managed to translate Trump's off-the-cuff word-salad speeches into a series of substantively awful policies and initiatives—mostly via executive orders that provoked intense liberal backlashes. This delighted Bannon, but disappointed the president, who wanted the American people to love him unconditionally, the way he loved himself.

After a protracted period, during which Bannon, Reince Priebus and Jared Kushner were all competing to serve as Trump's chief of staff, Bannon was ultimately ousted when the president appointed a man with some vague idea of how a chain of command works, the former four-star general John Kelly. While Kelly couldn't stop Trump behaving like a millennial and expressing every half-formed thought on social media, he could fire underlings who opposed him, like Bannon.

After Bannon's departure from the White House, his relationship with Trump soured when Michael Wolff's book *Fire And Fury* reported his scathing comments about the president—which did much to restore Bannon's reputation as an insightful political analyst.

Early life and education

Steve Bannon was born on 27 November 1953, and even though this was quite a long time ago, he's nowhere near as old as he looks. He was born into a pro-union working-class Irish Catholic family who were fans of the Kennedys, and whom he must have wanted to disappoint.

During his college years, the young Bannon worked at a junkyard, and was so filthy on returning home that his mother made him rinse himself outdoors with a hose. However, he grew to enjoy the sensation of being caked with dirt, and subsequently cultivated a dishevelled appearance, although he's careful never to appear so dirty that it's not obvious that he's white.

Bannon has degrees in urban planning and national security, as well as an MBA with honours from Harvard, making him the least unqualified member of Trump's initial West Wing team. He is the only MBA graduate in the history of Harvard not to believe in free trade.

Naval service

Bannon spent seven years as a naval officer; his time on the destroyer USS *Paul F. Foster* left him with a lifelong interest in destroying things.

He was part of Operation Eagle Claw—Jimmy Carter's failed attempt to end the Iran hostage crisis—which was partly foiled by sand, a not-unforeseeable element of a desert operation. Bannon has said that the mission's failure turned him into a Reaganite, and his belief that the best presidents are former entertainers suffering from dementia is what ultimately led him to join the Trump campaign.

Business career

Like every other White House staffer, Bannon once worked at Goldman Sachs. In 1990, he launched Bannon & Company, a boutique investment bank specialising in the media, which at one point handled the sale of production company Castle Rock. As part of his fee, he took a financial stake in *Seinfeld* and profits every time it's aired, which is officially the least funny thing about the show.

Later in the 1990s, he began producing Hollywood movies, beginning with standard fare like Sean Penn's *The Indian Runner,* but soon shifting away from Hollywood liberals and/or Indians to produce a series of alt-right documentaries. These included *Fire from the Heartland*, *Clinton Cash* and *Border War: The Battle Over Illegal Immigration*, as well as his greatest cinematic triumph, the unintentionally comic *Torchbearer*, in which the aged and bearded survivalist patriarch from the reality show *Duck Dynasty* shares his theories on religion.

Breitbart News

Bannon was a founding board member of Andrew Breitbart's alt-right news and opinion website and, after the founder's death in 2012, became executive chairman, taking the site in a bold new direction: even further to the right.

During Trump's election campaign in 2016, Breitbart began producing overtly white-supremacist content, much of it created by his protégé Milo Yiannopoulos, who was later fired from the site after it was discovered that he held pro-paedophilia views. This surprised critics who had doubted there was any problematic view the site was unwilling to embrace.

Bannon was also then a senior manager at Cambridge Analytica, the controversial data analytics provider that was, like Breitbart, partly owned by the Mercer family, and was, also like Breitbart, dragging the United States into a dystopian nightmare. Cambridge Analytica successfully co-opted the social media platforms created by globalist liberal tech geniuses in Silicon Valley to elect a white nationalist tariff enthusiast whose only interaction with communications technology comes in the form of angry tweets and a Sharpie.

Political career

On 17 August 2016, Bannon was appointed chief executive of Trump's campaign, ratifying the role he had essentially been playing from within Breitbart. He had the distinction of being the only senior figure within the campaign to genuinely believe Trump would beat Hillary Clinton, making him either a political genius or an idiot who could not understand polls but got lucky—or most likely, both.

After Trump's victory, he was named chief strategist and senior counsellor to the president-elect, although he was not tasked with offering the kind of counselling that Donald Trump most needs. Six days later, Bannon told the *Hollywood Reporter** that 'darkness is good', constituting the only time he has endorsed anything non-white. He explained: 'Dick Cheney. Darth Vader. Satan. That's power. It only helps us when [liberals] get it wrong. When they're blind to who we are and what we're doing.'

Such sentiments from a senior White House staffer shocked many, but Bannon also won praise for his unconventionally honest approach in not even pretending to do good.

In the months that followed, Bannon's stated admiration for Satan and, more disturbing still, Dick Cheney, would be borne out†.

Along with fellow alt-right apparatchik Stephen Miller, Bannon drafted Executive Order 13769, which looked like a Muslim ban, and had the practical effect of a Muslim ban, but was not, according to the administration, a Muslim ban. This claim was later rejected by a judge who deferred to Donald Trump's own campaign speeches in which he repeatedly described it as a Muslim ban. The Supreme Court later upheld the ban courtesy of Neil Gorsuch, the man Trump appointed to take the seat that should have been filled under President Obama, but which Republicans stole as part of their program of upholding American traditions.

Tension crept into Bannon's relationship with President Trump when the chief strategist appeared on the cover of *Time*, accompanied by a story suggesting that Bannon might be the second most powerful man in the

---

* Specifically, the *Hollywood Reporter* columnist Michael Wolff, a friendship that would later come back to bite him.

† By contrast, his admiration of Darth Vader seems ill-formed, given the ending of *Return of the Jedi*.

world. Awkwardly, this was a position Trump believed he himself held, behind Vladimir Putin.*

Departure

At his apex, Bannon was appointed a member of the National Security Council (NSC), an unprecedented position for someone in a political strategy role. However, he only attended one meeting before the council was restructured to explicitly exclude him—evidently others were more adept at strategy than he was.

The ousting of Reince Priebus as chief of staff in favour of John Kelly ended Bannon's direct access to Trump. Kelly was also opposed to Bannon's NSC role. Bannon was rumoured to have threatened to

Steve Bannon, former chief strategist to President Trump and current argument for moisturising. *(Gage Skidmore)*

quit if he was removed from the NSC, but ultimately the conflict was resolved in August 2017 when Bannon was either fired or resigned, depending on whom you ask.

---

* Some of Trump's golf properties display a fake cover of *Time* magazine boasting about his success, saying 'TRUMP IS HITTING ON ALL FRONTS . . . EVEN TV!' It was commissioned before it was plausible that he would genuinely appear on the cover thanks to his unlikely political triumph.

Bannon later claimed he'd only ever intended to stay with Trump for a year, but coincidentally ended up departing in the wake of the Charlottesville riot, after which he had notoriously counselled the president to say that there had been violence on 'many sides'. That he thought this was good advice illustrates why so few in the West Wing or the broader community mourned his departure.

The sudden exit of Steve Bannon meant that at least one white supremacist was punished in the immediate wake of Charlottesville.

Aftermath

As with other sudden White House departures, Bannon's abrupt exit seemed not to harm his close relationship with his former boss, with whom he still spoke frequently by phone. However, this symbiotic relationship between two thrice-married rich men who had really let themselves go soured instantly upon the publication of Michael Wolff's *Fire and Fury*, which featured several quotes in which Bannon broke the fundamental rule of remaining friends with the president—never offer anyone in the media your real, unfettered opinion of Trump.

John Barron

John Barron was a Trump spokesman, Trump executive and Trump representative in numerous media articles from 1980 until his abrupt disappearance in 1990. Barron frequently responded to requests for public comment on behalf of the supposedly extremely busy Trump, and his name has appeared in the *Washington Post*, *New York Times* and *New York* magazine, among other respected publications.

Barron was in a unique position to share insider information about Trump with the media, as he was none other than Trump himself.

Barron—spelled 'Baron' initially—first appeared in public in a 1980 *New York Times* article, when he commented on Trump's notorious demolition of art deco sculptures destined for the Metropolitan Museum of Art.

Among his many subsequent media appearances, 'Barron' helpfully:
- informed the press Trump had decided not to purchase the Cleveland Indians
- claimed that Trump's abandonment of a plan to build a replica castle, with moat and drawbridge, on Madison Avenue was a personal choice, rather than driven by the negative response from financiers and planning authorities
- urged fellow football owners in the US Football League to reimburse Trump for an expensive player
- lied to a *Forbes* reporter that Trump owned his father's assets in an attempt to get Trump on their rich list
- warned that workers who had sued Trump for underpayment might be countersued.

The latter incident spelled John Barron's demise, as in 1990 Trump was compelled to admit to using the alias in the resulting court case. But another John quickly materialised as Trump's preferred spokes-sock-puppet.

John Miller

In a phone interview with *People* magazine in 1991, 'Miller' explained why Trump dumped Marla Maples for Carla Bruni, the Italian model who would go on to marry another president. 'He really didn't want to make a commitment, he's coming out of a marriage, and he's starting to do tremendously well financially,' Miller said. He went on to explain that Trump was 'a good guy, and he's not going to hurt anybody', that 'actresses just call to see if they can go out with him and things', and that as well as living with Maples, Trump had 'three other girlfriends'.

During the 2016 campaign, the *Washington Post* obtained a tape of the interview and asked Trump whether he had ever employed a spokesman called John Miller, whereupon the phone went dead. Trump later denied being Miller, but the recording is available online, and it's either Trump, or an even more highly skilled impersonator than Alec Baldwin.

David Dennison

This was the alias Trump used for the non-disclosure agreement that Michael Cohen negotiated between Trump and Stormy Daniels aka Stephanie Clifford aka Peggy Peterson. Curiously, Cohen organised another 'hush agreement' involving a David Dennison: a $1.6 million payment to a *Playboy* model who was supposedly impregnated by high-profile Republican donor Elliott Broidy.

Another David Dennison, who is a 58-year-old importer of car accessories from Mendham, New Jersey, has clarified in an interview with *People* magazine that he has nothing to do with either case, and would like to know how they came up with his name.

Mr Green

Donald Trump's father, Fred, frequently used the alias 'Mr Green' to contact the media or fellow developers, which may have given his son the idea for John Barron. He is the only Green in the Trump family.

Legacy

Trump later paid his youngest son the ultimate compliment by naming the child after himself: Barron Trump. Trump has also suggested that John Miller might be able to serve as the White House communications director, in which role he would be more likely to succeed than Anthony Scaramucci.

Barron Trump

Barron William Trump is the youngest acknowledged son of Donald Trump. His mother is Melania Trump. As a minor, he is the only non-complicit member of the Trump family.

Being named after Donald Trump's imaginary spokesperson, as embarrassing as it must be, has to be better than being called Donald Trump Junior.

Battery theory

The **battery theory** was devised by Donald Trump, who postulated that humans are born with a finite amount of energy, like a battery, meaning that indulging in exercise unnecessarily wastes the remaining portion. This theory combines Trump's habitual rejection of science in favour of the bizarre emanations of his own brain (or gut)* with his strong desire

---

* The current appearance of said gut can be directly linked to Trump's belief in the 'battery theory'.

to avoid physical exercise. (Although he is allegedly more than willing to deplete his limited battery supply by spending time in the company of ladies with prominent modelling careers, or who have featured in *Playboy*, or starred in pornographic movies.)

An exhaustive fact-check by the renowned myth-debunking website Snopes.com has determined that, in fact, the human body is not at all like a battery with a finite amount of energy. Which is fortunate, as their investigation was a waste of energy.

Bill of Rights

The **Bill of Rights** is the collective term for the first ten amendments to the US Constitution. Taken together, they grant rights to citizens that supersede all other laws or decrees made by Congress or the president.

Though previously considered universal in their application, they have been reinterpreted under the Trump Administration as follows:

First amendment

Congress shall make no law respecting an establishment of religion, or prohibiting the free exercise thereof; or abridging the freedom of speech, or of the press; or the right of the people peaceably to assemble, and to petition the Government for a redress of grievances.

Donald J. Trump is to enjoy total free speech without consequences, but everybody else's speech about the president is to be policed closely, and especially that of female comedians like Kathy Griffin and Samantha Bee.

In particular, the media must not print anything that Donald Trump does not agree with, or portrays him in a negative light, or that he designates as 'fake news' on the Official People's Twitter Account, @realDonaldTrump.

The right of the people peaceably to assemble is to be preserved, unless they are ethnic types turning an American city into a 'no-go area', in which case the police should shoot to kill.

Any count issued by the White House press secretary of the number of the people peaceably assembling to attend any particular event may not be challenged.

Finally, while no laws respecting religion will be passed, laws disrespecting certain religions are allowed. Preventing adherents of one particular religion from entering the United States is to be permitted on grounds of national security and/or bigotry.

Second amendment

A well regulated Militia, being necessary to the security of a free State, the right of the people to keep and bear Arms, shall not be infringed.

This is the most important amendment, and operates to the exclusion of all others. While it may lead to mass shootings, those who die will be happy to go to their graves knowing that they were upholding a principle based on weapons technology from 1789.

Militia groups supportive of the president are actively encouraged, and in the event of any violent conflict, it will be officially noted by the commander-in-chief that there were good people on both sides.

Third amendment

No Soldier shall, in time of peace be quartered in any house, without the consent of the Owner, nor in time of war, but in a manner to be prescribed by law.

US military around the world will be accommodated, at the government's expense, at the nearest Trump property.

Fourth amendment

The right of the people to be secure in their persons, houses, papers, and effects, against unreasonable searches and seizures, shall not be violated, and no Warrants shall issue, but upon probable cause, supported by Oath or affirmation, and particularly describing the place to be searched, and the persons or things to be seized.

It is now assumed that this amendment was intended to apply in the case of the Greatest Witch Hunt in American History, otherwise known as Special Counsel Robert Mueller's bogus investigation, which is unlawful and unconstitutional and just plain unfair.

In particular, the hotel suite of the president's personal lawyer is not to be raided while searching for evidence of any payments to any porn stars that the president has already denied making.

Nor is anyone to search the bank account records of any company established for the purpose of making payments to porn stars, or receiving dubious payments from well-known American companies and Russian billionaires who are close personal mates of Vladimir Putin.

However, the tax returns of the president of the United States will be treated as sacrosanct, and need never be released. Anyone querying this will be told that they are under audit, so there.

Fifth amendment

No person shall be held to answer for a capital, or otherwise infamous crime, unless on a presentment or indictment of a Grand Jury, except in cases arising in the land or naval forces, or in the Militia, when in actual service in time of War or public danger; nor shall any person be subject for the same offence to be twice put in jeopardy of life or limb; nor shall be compelled in any criminal case to be a witness against himself, nor be deprived of life, liberty, or property, without due process of law; nor shall private property be taken for public use, without just compensation.

No president shall ever be held to answer for any crime, and grand juries may not be assembled to investigate anything that they do. In particular, no president shall be made to answer any difficult questions about Russia, or porn stars, or Russian porn stars, lest they incriminate themselves. And nor shall any of their lawyers, associates or former lovers, or Sean Hannity.

Anyone whom the president pardons may not be tried for the same offence in a liberal state like New York.

Private property may be seized for public use if that public use is as a Trump hotel, resort or casino.

Sixth amendment

In all criminal prosecutions, the accused shall enjoy the right to a speedy and public trial, by an impartial jury of the State and district wherein the crime shall have been committed, which district shall have been previously ascertained by law, and to be informed of the nature and cause of the accusation; to be confronted with the witnesses against him; to have compulsory process for obtaining witnesses in his favour, and to have the Assistance of Counsel for his defence.

Unless they are Crooked Hillary Clinton, who is guilty. Lock her up!

Seventh amendment

In Suits at common law, where the value in controversy shall exceed twenty dollars, the right of trial by jury shall be preserved, and no fact tried by a jury, shall be otherwise re-examined in any Court of the United States, than according to the rules of the common law.

Said jury is to be made up of members of the Trump family, gathered at Trump Tower in a 'boardroom' containing television cameras and broadcast live on television, after which one of those on trial is to be told, 'You're fired!'

Eight amendment

Excessive bail shall not be required, nor excessive fines imposed, nor cruel and unusual punishments inflicted.

Torture is no longer considered cruel and unusual, but instead useful and effective, and encouraged wherever possible. It may be used at Guantanamo Bay, on American soil, or in the top-secret overseas prison to which Jeff Bezos will shortly be renditioned via a disguised CIA flight unless his lying newspaper stops printing fake news about the president.

Being forced to watch all fourteen seasons of *The Apprentice* hosted by Donald J. Trump may not be deemed a cruel and unusual punishment, but being made to watch the season hosted by Arnold Schwarzenegger is.

Ninth amendment

The enumeration in the Constitution, of certain rights, shall not be construed to deny or disparage others retained by the people.

However, the right to disparage others will be restricted for exclusive use of the president.

Tenth amendment

The powers not delegated to the United States by the Constitution, nor prohibited by it to the States, are reserved to the States respectively, or to the people.

Specifically one of 'the people', President Donald J. Trump, or if he is incapacitated in any way, Ivanka.

Birtherism

Birtherism is the practice of raising questions about a president's place of birth, and refusing to accept evidence that conclusively proves they were born in the United States, and are therefore eligible for the office.

For example, some people are not convinced Donald Trump was born in America. In fact, it's possible that Donald Trump was born in his mother's country of origin, Scotland—the evidence that Trump was born in America is dubious, and could have been Photoshopped, so lots of people are talking about it. Consequently, nobody can be completely sure that Donald Trump was born in the United States, which would mean he is not eligible to be president of the United States.

To reiterate—he is not eligible to be president of the United States. In other words, Donald Trump is not a legitimate president.

If people's suspicions are correct, that is. And many, many people are not convinced.

Alternatively, Trump might have been born in Germany, where his grandfather was born. Trump has many values that have historically been associated with that country, rather than the America that elected Barack Obama. Authoritarianism, white nationalism, trashing existing institutions and a charismatic leader who says things like, 'I am your voice', and 'I alone can fix it'—these things conjure up memories of a particular period in German history.

Can Americans be sure that someone who behaves like he might have been born in Germany shares their American values? Many people are saying no.

As a final example, Trump's own birth certificate, we are assured, says he was born in Jamaica. This is an area of Queens, New York City, but it's also a country in the Caribbean. It would be so easy for people in the Deep State who hate America to modify Trump's birth certificate so it said 'Jamaica, New York' instead of just 'Jamaica'. It's much easier to add text to a birth certificate than remove it, and there are YouTube videos demonstrating this, some of which have as many as dozens of views. In other words, we cannot be sure that Donald Trump was not born in a country where most people have African ancestry. People are talking about this.

Perhaps if Donald Trump releases his long-form birth certificate, the American people will be able to feel confident that he is eligible for the presidency—but even then, birth certificates can be falsified. Again, it's on YouTube.

In summary, Americans may never know whether this president is legitimate. It is not such a long bow to draw to conclude that he should not be president at all

Cabinet

(Correct at the time of writing, but subject to constant, unpredictable change.)

Alexander Acosta, Labor Secretary—The only Hispanic member of Trump's Cabinet to date, with extensive experience in the field, Acosta was obviously not Trump's first choice for the role of labor secretary. But when fast-food CEO Andrew Puzder was unable to be confirmed for the job of keeping the pay packets of the minimum-wage employees who work in his businesses as low as possible, Trump was willing to settle for Acosta.

The Trump Cabinet in March 2017, before several rounds of purges. The boom microphones are for the convenience of Russian intelligence. *(Office of the President of the United States, Donald Trump/Twitter)*

Alex Azar, Secretary of Health and Human Services—Unsurprisingly, Trump's nominee to run the US health system is a former lawyer and drug company executive with no medical training. Like Trump, Azar opposes abortion and Obamacare, but has not been able to articulate a viable alternative to the latter.

Ben Carson, Secretary of Housing and Urban Development—If one imagines that the challenge of managing HUD is exactly like performing an operation on a child with a brain tumour, then the brilliant paediatric neurosurgeon Carson is the man for the job. But when one considers that HUD is nothing whatsoever like a child with a brain tumour, one can readily understand why Carson is doing a poor job. As one of the most complicated agencies, HUD would have benefited from a secretary with considerable experience in public service—or indeed any. (*See also* **Republican primaries, 2016**)

Elaine Chao, Secretary of Transportation—Rather awkwardly, Chao is married to Senate Majority Leader and frequent Trump punching bag Mitch McConnell. Trump has asked Chao to investigate transportation in the Australian sense: deporting people he considers criminals to other countries. Crooked Hillary is to be sent to Zanzibar.

Daniel Coats, Director of National Intelligence—Coats has extensive experience as a former member of both houses of Congress, as well as the Senate intelligence committee. He was also the US ambassador to Germany, and has served in the US Army. It's genuinely surprising that Trump chose somebody so well qualified for such an important role.

Betsy DeVos, Secretary of Education—DeVos's appointment was based on Trump's assumption that to oversee academic excellence, his nominee doesn't necessarily need any herself—or experience as an educator, as opposed to as an agitator. As a long-term supporter of a voucher policy, which would inject parental choice into the public school system, she should, in the interests of consistency, offer parents a voucher that allows them to move their children to a more qualified education secretary.

Nikki Haley, US Representative to the UN—Having initially carved out a separate position on several key foreign policy issues from Rex Tillerson, and then from President Trump himself, she is the most likely Cabinet member to run against her boss in the Republican primaries.

Gina Haspel, Director of the Central Intelligence Agency—Haspel is the first woman to hold the role, but far from the first torturer. She ran a 'black site' in Thailand where prisoners were subjected to so-called 'enhanced interrogation techniques', which was a means of inflicting physical violence on detainees to ensure the intelligence they provided was absolutely useless.

John Kelly, Chief of Staff—He has the hardest job of anybody on this list: making the Cabinet process run efficiently when its members are these people, and Donald Trump. (*See also* **John Kelly**)

Robert Lighthizer, US Trade Representative—Previously deputy trade representative under President Reagan, who was predominantly a free-trader and the original initiator of NAFTA, Lighthizer's priorities under Trump are now the exact opposite.

James Mattis, Secretary of Defense—His primary duty is suggesting that President Trump hold off from any spontaneous plan for invasion. (*See also* **James Mattis**)

Linda McMahon, Administrator of the Small Business Administration—McMahon comes to this position from the WWE, which makes her appointment both hilarious and more appropriate than many of Trump's selections, as she does have experience running a successful business. It does, however, raise the concerning possibility that Trump thinks a major entertainment conglomerate counts as a 'small business'.

Steven Mnuchin, Treasury Secretary—As treasury secretary, his major accomplishments have been passing tax reform that overwhelmingly benefits rich people like himself and spending a gobsmacking amount of government money on military flights, including two $300,000 flights to Europe and a one-hour flight from Washington to New York that cost $25,000. Mnuchin even requested a government aircraft to fly him to Europe for his honeymoon. Despite his current role running the US economy, his all-time career highlight remains being an executive producer of *The Lego Movie*.

Mick Mulvaney, Director of the Office of Management and Budget—
Mulvaney famously said of his time in Congress, 'If you are a lobbyist who never gave us money, I did not talk to you. If you are a lobbyist who gave us money, I might talk to you.' He is considered unlikely to help President Trump 'drain the swamp'.

Kirstjen Nielsen, Secretary of Homeland Security—Although notionally her top priority is to secure the homeland by coordinating the seventeen US security agencies, Nielsen currently spends most of her time being berated by President Trump for failing to build The Wall that under no circumstances will ever be built. More recently, she has had the job of explaining to the American people why separating children from their parents at the border is humane, necessary for national security and the Democrats' fault, and then why her department isn't going to do it anymore.

Rick Perry, Energy Secretary—A somewhat surprising choice, as not only had he run against Trump, and then endorsed Ted Cruz, but he previously advocated the abolition of the department he now runs. This occurred during his 2012 presidential campaign, when he made one of the greatest debate gaffes of all time, declaring he wanted to abolish three departments but only being able to name two of them. Energy was the one he forgot.

To Perry, the energy secretary should be the coal secretary: he said in 2017 that burning fossil fuels could reduce sexual assault in places like Africa, as it would provide 'light that shines the righteousness, if you will, on those types of acts'. Experts say that there isn't necessarily a link between electric light and reduced rates of assault—presumably all the locations where Donald Trump spontaneously grabbed the genitalia of various women had electric lighting.

Perry does not believe in climate change, and has previously expressed scepticism towards evolution. Conversely, many people do not believe in Rick Perry. (*See also* **Republican primaries, 2016**)

Mike Pence, Vice President—His job in Cabinet meetings is to say 'Yes, Mr President' a lot, while plotting to take his boss's job. (See also **Mike Pence**.)

Sonny Perdue, Secretary of Agriculture—A veterinarian by trade, and former governor of Georgia, he was one of the least controversial Trump nominees. Perdue passed tough anti-immigrant measures as governor, which is perhaps what endeared him to Trump. With a personal fortune of $6 million, he is one of Trump's poorest Cabinet members.

Mike Pompeo, Secretary of State—Rex Tillerson's replacement as diplomat-in-chief has so far spent much of his time in largely fruitless negotiations with North Korea and reassuring key allies that President Trump doesn't really mean what he says.

Wilbur Ross, Commerce Secretary—This investor, nicknamed the 'King of Bankruptcy' for his ability to turn struggling companies around, is the perfect official to help run the hideously indebted US economy. He once helped Trump refinance one of his disastrous casinos, however, so his record isn't perfect.

Jeff Sessions, Attorney General—Although he gave up his Senate seat to take up the role, Sessions almost immediately lost the confidence of President Trump after recusing himself from the Russia investigation on the entirely justifiable basis that he had not only met with the Russian ambassador during the campaign, but failed to declare it during his confirmation hearing. The president now openly regrets hiring Sessions, reflecting Trump's perception that the role of his Justice Department is to protect him personally, rather than the Constitution and laws of the United States.

Sessions' expertise in being unable to protect people has been highlighted via his implementation of the administration's strict border policy, where he has delighted in the administration's unwillingness to protect children from being separated from their parents. Sessions has argued that the policy is Biblical on the basis of a misinterpretation of Jesus' well-known statement 'suffer the little children'.

Ryan Zinke, Secretary of the Interior—Zinke's major involvement with the US interior has been shooting at it, which, as a former Navy SEAL, he's very good at. He sought to remove the ban on importing elephant 'trophies'—that is, parts of elephants shot during overseas

Interior Secretary Zinke prefers bullets that penetrate wild animals' interiors.

hunting expeditions—but in a rare display of taste, President Trump overruled him.

On his first day, Zinke cancelled the Obama administration's ban on lead bullets and fishing tackle, making it easier for lead to travel into the interior of the animals in our food supply. Zinke has also devoted considerable time to declassifying and shrinking national parks, and increasing his department's travel allowance.

Cameos by Donald Trump

Donald Trump has appeared in many movies and television programs as himself, including:

Home Alone 2: Lost In New York (1992)—Macauley Culkin is lost in the iconic Plaza Hotel, then owned by Trump, who pops up to tell him how to get to the lobby. At the time, Trump was making his own losses in his Atlantic City casinos.

The Fresh Prince of Bel-Air (1994)—The Donald turns up at the Banks house and is mistakenly thought to be a prospective buyer. Trump was willing to appear on Will Smith's hit television show despite it featuring a property inhabited by African-Americans.

Pizza Hut commercial (1994, and beyond)—Trump appeared in multiple commercials over the years because he loves publicity even more than he loves pizza and/or huts.

The Nanny (1997)—Trump played himself, as a rich friend of Nanny Fran whom she was using to make Mr Sheffield jealous. Trump took a call on a mobile phone, said, 'I told you not to call me on this line again,' then pulled out a phone from his other pocket, saying, 'That's better.' It's not clear whether the call was from Stormy Daniels.

In the 1990s, Donald Trump's casino problems made his fortune almost as fictitious as Mr Sheffield's. *(CBS)*

The Drew Carey Show (1997)—Trump finds Drew Carey and his friends on the street, and offers them free tickets to the Yankees. Knowing Trump's practices, they would most likely have been tickets that had been donated to the Trump Foundation.

Spin City (1998)—Michael J. Fox's political spin doctor character introduces Donald Trump as an author, which was intended as a laugh line. Had he introduced him as a future president of the United States, there would have been a considerably bigger laugh.

Sex and the City (1998)—Trump appeared on the show multiple times, as a human symbol of New York. Implausibly, his character did not have sex with Samantha.

Zoolander (2001)—Trump appears in the red carpet montage praising Derek Zoolander, without whom 'male modelling wouldn't be what it is today'. This claim is fake news.

McDonald's commercial (2002)—Donald Trump can't believe the amazing deal that is a Big N' Tasty Burger for one dollar, so he asks Grimace how he does it. Grimace says nothing, presumably because he's concerned that the conversation is under surveillance by Robert Mueller.

Two Weeks Notice (2002)—Trump hassles his fellow plutocrat Hugh Grant, and threatens to poach his general counsel. This feels credible given the rapid rate at which Trump goes through lawyers.

Century 21 commercial (2012)—In a Super Bowl ad, Trump gets out-negotiated by a Century 21 real-estate agent whose business skills he can't believe. This agent might have been the one who sold him those casinos.

Presidential campaign (2015 to present)—His most extensive cameo yet, as a legitimate politician.

Trump casinos

The main hotel–casino complexes owned by Donald Trump during his 25 years of doing business in Atlantic City were the **Trump Taj Mahal**, the **Trump Plaza** and the **Trump Marina**. But despite the considerable publicity Trump's casinos attracted, the operating company filed for bankruptcy in 2004, 2009 and 2014, because the long-time gaming industry maxim that 'The house always wins' does not apply when the house is owned by Donald Trump.

Trump's publicly listed business—Trump Hotel & Casino Resorts—managed to lose money every year from when it was floated in 1995 to its final bankruptcy in 2004. CNN calculated that an investor in his stock—which traded, of course, under the symbol DJT—who had put in $100 at the float would have had $8.77 by the time it went bankrupt.

Trump himself lost $647 million, while Carl Icahn, who bailed out the business after its final bankruptcy, lost $100 million. Inexplicably, the episode did not permanently dent Trump's reputation as a business genius.

History

Trump Plaza

Trump's first application for a casino licence was approved in 1982, but while planning his own project, he was invited to run a hotel–casino project for Harrah's, the gaming brand owned by the Holiday Inn. Despite Harrah's budget image, Trump built 85 high-roller suites that were rarely used, damaging the profitability of the casino. Two years after its 1984 opening, Trump bought the property and renamed it the Trump Plaza Hotel and Casino.

The property had the honour of hosting Wrestlemania in 1988 and 1989, but ran into financial difficulty the following year after Trump opened the larger Taj Mahal. The Plaza only avoided a financial default by mortgaging its own parking garage—the business equivalent of selling a kidney for another spin of the roulette wheel.

Trump eventually managed the property out of its financial strife, and began expanding in 1993, only to be thwarted by his inability to eject a retired homeowner so he could use her property for limousine parking.

In 1995, Trump transferred ownership of the hotel to his new listed company, Trump Hotels & Casino Resorts, which continued to expand the site, adding the Trump World's Fair Casino to the Trump Regency Hotel that he had already purchased. The casino had nothing whatsoever in common with the altruistic, high-tech vision of the future showcased at a regular World's Fair.

In 2011, Trump announced that he wanted to find a buyer for the Plaza, but could not, so it was announced in July 2014 that the casino would close in September if a buyer could not be found. Then in August, Trump filed a lawsuit to get his name removed from the property, which by then was subject to yet another licensing deal.

No buyer could found, so the casino closed on 16 September. Demolition is planned for 2018.

Trump Marina

The casino was initially built by Hilton Hotels, which had its gambling licence rejected by New Jersey authorities due to alleged links with organised crime. Consequently, the property was sold to the supposedly much cleaner Donald Trump, who opened it in 1985 as Trump's Castle. In 1990, it became the setting for *Trump Card*, a television game show based on bingo that was cancelled after one season despite featuring a priceless promotional appearance from Donald Trump in its first episode.

Despite the marketing bonanza of *Trump Card* that same year, however, the casino also began struggling once the Trump Taj Mahal opened in 1990, and achieved saturation in the 'casino in Atlantic City named after Donald Trump' market.

In December that year, the casino was only able to make a payment to bondholders because Fred Trump bought $3.5 million in chips. Though it was later determined to be an illegal loan, the fine was merely 1 per cent of the amount Trump's father had put in, and the casino stayed afloat.

Afloat, that is, until the next payment was due. It began restructuring its debt in May 1991. Trump rejected Hilton's offer to buy the casino back—rather optimistically, when he already had two other casinos on the strip—and successfully refinanced to give his bondholders 50 per cent ownership. He bought it back the following year, then sold it to his publicly traded company in 1996.

Shortly afterwards, Trump considered a deal to rebrand the Castle as a Hard Rock Hotel and Casino, but instead of a Hard Rock, he chose a hard place, and rebranded it as Trump Marina. It continued to struggle, and was ultimately taken over by Trump's bondholders after the company's 2009 bankruptcy.

Ultimately the property was purchased by Landry's for just $38 million in 2011, and renamed the Golden Nugget. It is now the base for a highly profitable online casino site, GoldenNuggetCasino.com.

The roof of the casino hosts a radio transmitter that broadcasts a Christian rock station.

Trump Taj Mahal

Trump acquired most of the company that had already started building the casino in 1986, after the death of its founder. Its initial budget had been $250 million, but the cost eventually blew out to $930 million. Trump offered the remaining shareholders a buyout, but ended up competing against television legend Merv Griffin—both men ended up suing each other. Ultimately a deal was done, and it opened in 1990.

Trump's Taj Mahal was somewhat less religious than the original.

The Indian-themed Trump Taj Mahal claimed to be the largest casino in the world, and was later the home of Scores*, America's first casino-based strip club.

The following year, even though the Taj Mahal had driven both the Plaza and the Castle to the wall, Trump's latest property hit financial strife itself. Like the other two properties, Trump took it through a structured bankruptcy. The casino had proven so expensive to construct that it drove all three Trump properties into financial difficulty.

---

* Continuing the brand's association with political leaders, its sister property in Manhattan was famously visited by Kevin Rudd shortly before he became prime minister.

Though it was struggling to attract enough customers, federal authorities later revealed that the Taj Mahal had considerable success in attracting Russian mobsters from Brooklyn. The casino was frequently investigated for money laundering, and paid a $10 million fine in 2015. The US Treasury—which Trump now runs—found that the Trump Taj Mahal had failed to take sufficient precautions to prevent money laundering, despite repeatedly being warned about the crimes committed on its premises. There were also many investigations into the casino's links with organised crime, including one by the US Senate that named individuals with Triad links.

Trump Entertainment Resorts, the public company that had purchased all of Trump's casinos in 1996, filed for bankruptcy in 2014 and Trump Taj Mahal nearly closed. Now a subsidy of Carl Icahn's company in which Trump no longer holds any shares, Trump Entertainment Resorts exited bankruptcy in February 2016, but ultimately closed the Taj Mahal on 10 October 2016, less than a month before Trump's election victory. Three thousand people lost their jobs with the final failure of Trump's white elephant (which rather bravely featured statues of white elephants out the front), but, as with so much of the negative publicity about Trump that emerged during the campaign, it had no impact on his popularity.

The Hard Rock Cafe in the building has remained open, however, and its parent company ultimately purchased the entire complex, and will soon reopen it as an extensively remodelled Hard Rock Hotel and Casino. Unlike its namesake, Trump's Taj Mahal is not World Heritage-listed.

Other businesses

Trump also owned casinos in Gary, Indiana, and Coachella, California. Nowadays, however, his only gambling enterprise is the economy of the United States.

The casino is fronted by metaphors for the project once dubbed the 'eighth wonder of the world'. *(Mark Goebel/Flickr)*

Legacy

Clearly, Trump enjoyed playing the part of the flamboyant casino owner, but the part of the role where you obsessively check the books to make sure each part of the business is generating profit seems to have had limited interest for him—bearing in mind that he ran many other businesses at the same time and remained in New York City rather than relocating to Atlantic City.

The way Trump told it on the campaign trail, he made lots of money from Atlantic City and left at just the right time. It's not clear whether this is true, given that he hasn't released his tax returns. If not, he wouldn't be the first person to take a financial bath in Atlantic City. Generally, though, those who do are gamblers rather than the people who own the house.

Charlottesville rally

The **Charlottesville rally**, which began on 11 August 2017, was a conflict that resulted in three deaths and 38 injuries, after far-right groups marched to protest the removal of a statue of Confederate general Robert E. Lee, and also express their lingering resentment that their side lost the Civil War.

The event proved challenging for the president of the United States, who struggled to definitively attribute blame. The 'Unite The Right' protesters were an assortment of white supremacists, nationalists, Ku Klux Klan members, militia members, neo-Confederates and neo-Nazis, but the leader of the free world pointed out that there was 'hatred, bigotry and violence on many sides', and that both sides had 'very fine people'. Others felt that if a fatal conflict's clear instigators are swastika-wielding self-identified Nazis marching through a small town by torchlight[*] to frighten their political opponents, the side deserving condemnation is reasonably clear.

Many expressed surprise at President Trump's moral ambivalence. Conventional politicians and commentators were shocked that Trump could equivocate in the aftermath of a violent Nazi rally on US soil, while Trump's supporters were surprised he thought there were any 'fine people' among the Antifa demonstrators.

A specially convened United Nations panel condemned Trump's unwillingness to 'unequivocally reject and condemn racist violence'. In response, President Trump and his supporters unequivocally rejected and condemned the United Nations.

---

[*] The torches were in a tiki style available at Home Depot, meaning that the attempt to invoke white supremacy paid inadvertent tribute to Polynesian culture.

Christian right

The **Christian right**, in terms of US politics, is a political faction known for its support of social conservatism. Made up primarily of right-wing evangelical Protestants and conservative Catholics, the Christian right is known for its hardline positions in policy areas like school prayer, contraception, abortion, homosexuality, evolution, euthanasia and pornography.

Usually members of the Christian right are inflexible in their religious dogma, but in the case of Donald Trump a special exception has been made. Because while Trump is a greedy, selfish, philandering, insulting, lying, multiple-divorcee braggart known for crotch-grabbing, at least he's not a Democrat.

Hillary Clinton

Hillary Rodham Clinton is the person a significant majority of Americans chose to be the 45th president of the United States. She won more votes than any candidate ever, and as a former first lady, senator and secretary of state, she was one of the most experienced candidates in decades.

However, Clinton was careless with her personal email account during her time at the State Department, so ultimately lost the election to a guy whose most significant prior public service was signing Gary Busey for *The Celebrity Apprentice*.

2016 campaign

Throughout the campaign, Donald Trump referred to Clinton as 'Crooked Hillary', regularly led his rallies in frenzied chants of 'Lock her up!' and, in the second debate, loomed intimidatingly behind her while she was speaking—all perfectly reasonable in American public discourse.

Despite these tactics, had Clinton simply focused more on the swing states in recent presidential elections, instead of taking them for granted and diverting campaign expenditure to traditional red states like Arizona and Nevada, she would be president now.

Had FBI director James Comey publicly announced that Trump's campaign was under investigation for collusion with Russia in the same way he announced that Clinton was being investigated, she would be president now.

If Hillary Clinton or her team had remembered the slogan famously written on the wall of her husband's campaign headquarters, 'It's the economy, stupid', and paid more attention to those who were struggling because they'd slipped through the cracks, she might have made inroads into Trump's white, working-class base, many of them traditional Democrat voters, and she would be president now.

Or if 107,000 people in Michigan, Wisconsin and Pennsylvania had voted the other way, or if more Democrat supporters had turned out in those states she would be president now.

Or if white women had chosen to put one of their own in the Oval Office for the first time, instead of 53 per cent of them voting for a guy whose major 'women's issue' during the campaign was the revelation that he enjoyed randomly groping female strangers, she would be president now.

Or if the US electoral system didn't skew the presidential race, due to a system of rural gerrymandering known as the electoral college, she would be president now.

Then again, there were those emails. So in the end, can she really blame anyone but herself?*

It should also be noted that Trump doesn't know how to use email, and until the invention of Twitter, his main method of communication was the telephone he used to ring news organisations pretending to be his own publicist.

Roy Cohn

Roy Cohn (1927–1986) was a lawyer who worked for Donald Trump for many years, serving as something of a mentor to him. He was involved in the controversial trial of Julius and Ethel Rosenberg, which ended in their death sentence despite various improprieties during the trial, some of which Cohn was responsible for.

He was also Joseph McCarthy's chief counsel during his notorious investigations into communism. During that period he and McCarthy targeted prominent figures not just for their suspected links to communism, but for their homosexuality—many lost their jobs as a result. The campaign became known as the 'Lavender Scare', as it was based on the perception that communist agents had infiltrated the government by threatening to reveal powerful men's homosexuality in order to blackmail them. The fact

---

* Her book *What Happened* suggests that yes, she absolutely can.

that Cohn himself was gay seemed not to deter him from ruining other gay men's lives.

Trump began working with Cohn when his family company was in trouble with the government for refusing to rent properties to African-Americans or people on welfare. Under Cohn's tutelage, he countersued for $100 million, and while the suit failed, it taught him to always counterpunch harder, even when you're in the wrong.

Cohn also worked for Rupert Murdoch, and introduced him to Trump in the 1970s. The two moguls would later bond, as they had in common Murdoch's news channel, which thought that Donald Trump was amazing, and Donald Trump, who also thought that Donald Trump was amazing.

Roy Cohn was significantly responsible for the person Donald Trump eventually became, meaning that much of where we are today is his fault.

James Comey

James Brien[*] **Comey Junior** is the former director of the FBI, whose unfair vendetta destroyed Hillary Clinton's/Donald Trump's presidency. He was fired for his role investigating the email/Russia scandal.

Comey is a compromised lackey of the Republican/Democratic party who will always be notorious for his decision to reveal that Hillary Clinton had been under investigation/that Trump may have improperly pressured

---

[*] Comey's middle name is deliberately spelled with an 'e' to make it harder for hackers to guess the password he uses on every website, 'brian'.

Comey to abandon his investigation into Trump's first national security adviser, Michael Flynn.

This harm was compounded by Comey's decision to publicly announce that Clinton's investigation had been reopened because of materials found on Anthony Weiner's laptop/tell the Senate Intelligence Committee that he kept detailed notes of his meetings with the president because he thought Donald Trump would lie.

After slinking away from the FBI, Comey further tarnished his reputation by writing a book called *A Higher Loyalty*. In it, he explains that he would do it all again, a conclusion unlikely to win support from Clinton/ Trump supporters, who blame him for their preferred president's current predicament.

James Comey, Barack Obama and Robert Mueller, seen here in 2013 conspiring to destroy the presidency of Donald Trump. *(US Government)*

Covfefe

Covfefe is a neologism coined by, then shortly afterwards repudiated by, President Trump.

Origins

On 31 May 2017, Trump tweeted the words, 'Despite the constant negative press covfefe', without specifying what had been achieved despite it, or indeed what 'covfefe' was, and then fell silent for several hours. In this brief interregnum, social media users and every media outlet pondered what the word might mean, and speculated that the president might have suffered an aneurysm, or even died, mid tweet.

These few brief hours of playful speculation remain the happiest period of the Trump presidency. The utter joy felt by the many thousand Twitter users who joked about the word's possible meanings was in no way diminished by the fact that Trump was clearly trying to write the word 'coverage'.

Five hours later, Trump deleted what had already become one of the most popular tweets of the year and challenged his followers to guess what 'covfefe' meant in a rare and unsuccessful attempt at humour.

Aftermath

When subsequently asked about it, then-Press Secretary Sean Spicer claimed, apparently in earnest (although it was never easy to tell), that President Trump 'and a small group of people know exactly what he meant', implying the existence of a Covfefe Cabinet. This was unconvincing even by Spicer's standards, unless what had been meant was that Trump should stop tweeting while on the toilet.

Mike Quigley, a Democratic congressman for Illinois, reacted to the incident by proposing the *Communications Over Various Feeds Electronically for Engagement Act*, which would have preserved all of Trump's tweets in the National Archive, even the erroneous ones that he had deleted. Unfortunately, by the time the congressman had worked out a title for the bill that enabled its first letters to spell out the word covfefe, the whole phenomenon was no longer the least bit funny.

Stormy Daniels

Stephanie A. Gregory Clifford is known professionally as **Stormy Daniels**, Stormy Waters or simply Stormy. She's known in contracts as Peggy Peterson. And she's been known in the biblical sense by Donald J. Trump, president of the United States—allegedly.

She is a pornographic actress, stripper, screenwriter, director and litigant. During her time in the adult industry, Daniels has won many awards, including Favourite Breasts at the F.A.M.E. Awards in 2006, 2007 and 2009, which is apparently a real category.

Daniels' involvement in politics began before her current dispute with President Trump—after a campaign by fans in 2009, she announced she was running for the Senate in Louisiana as a Republican. Despite having previously been a Democrat, she had decided the Republican Party best reflected her libertarian views about sex, money, and sex for money.

Alleged relationship with Donald Trump

Stormy Daniels is alleged to have had alleged sex with Donald Alleged Trump allegedly in 2006, allegedly, which was her first year as Favourite Breasts laureate. In her conversation with the alleged Anderson Cooper on *60 Alleged Minutes* in 2018, she claimed that she met the alleged president at an alleged celebrity golf tournament in Lake Tahoe, and he invited her, allegedly, to his hotel alleged suite.

Apparently it's worth paying $130,000 not to have sex with this woman *(Glenn Francis, www. PacificProDigital.com)*

Donald Trump showed her his latest alleged magazine, with his alleged face on the cover, and Daniels allegedly asked whether these tactics usually worked for him, and suggested that somebody should spank him with his own alleged magazine. He then allegedly allowed her to do exactly allegedly that.

Daniel then alleges that Trump told her that she reminded him of Ivanka, which, though only alleged, does sound like the kind of thing that Donald Trump would allegedly say about his daughter. He suggested that Daniels could allegedly be a contestant on *The Alleged Apprentice*.

When she emerged from the bathroom, she alleged that Trump was sitting on the edge of the bed, apparently expecting them to have sex, and her alleged thought was, 'Ugh, here we go'—which again seems plausible. Allegedly.

Just before the 2016 election, in October, Daniels signed a non-disclosure agreement, not allegedly but actually, and was paid $130,000 by Trump's lawyer, Michael Cohen. Daniels also claims that she was physically threatened not to say anything about Trump.

According to Rudy Giuliani, Trump's newest lawyer, the president subsequently reimbursed Cohen for this payment. But Trump still denies that they had sex, because allegedly Donald Trump is so good at business that he sometimes pays people large sums of money to cover up things that didn't happen. Allegedly.

Legal fallout

After the *Wall Street Journal* reported on the existence of the non-disclosure agreement, Daniels sued Cohen and his client Trump to obtain a declaration that it was invalid. She also argued that it was never valid, because Trump never signed it. Daniels also subsequently sued Trump about his tweet that mocked her claims of being threatened. There are multiple other lawsuits between other women claiming to have allegedly been involved with Trump, and the special counsel has been looking into various interesting payments to a company set up by Michael Cohen and used to make the payment to Daniels.

Even on the basis of the undisputed facts, Cohen has questions to answer about a potential breach of campaign finance laws, and ethics rules about making loans to clients.

The massive public interest in these matters has had a significant impact on the careers of those involved. Stormy Daniels has embarked on a nationwide stripping tour under the banner 'Make America Horny Again', while her lawyer, Michael Avenatti, has been even more ubiquitous, albeit considerably less naked.

While the full facts of these affairs, both business and personal, are not yet known, it is indisputably the case that Stormy Daniels was paid $130,000, and that while this is a substantial sum of money, it is barely adequate compensation for any 27 year old who allegedly had to endure sex with a 60-year-old Donald Trump.

Deep state

The **deep state** refers to permanent decision-making bodies and centres of power within government that cannot be removed by a change of government, as well as powerful players like high finance and the upper echelons of industry. The deep state ultimately reduces the power of elected officials by forming a shadow government that endures no matter which party is in power.

The term's origins lie in describing situations in developing countries like Egypt, Pakistan and Turkey, where elites in the military and bureaucracies routinely ignore directions from elected officials, but it was first used extensively in reference to the United States by supporters of both Donald Trump and Bernie Sanders during their primary campaigns. The deep state would prevent presidents from achieving their agendas and deprive the American people of power in a thoroughly sinister fashion except for the fact that, in the United States at least, it simply doesn't exist.

Diet Coke

Among his many other achievements, Donald J. Trump is the world's most famous **Diet Coke** drinker. Trump has compensated for the unusual restraint he shows by choosing the sugar-free version, however, by drinking twelve cans a day. It's been reported that rather than deploying nuclear warheads, the red button on the president's desk is for ordering Diet Cokes.

The large amount of caffeine in Trump's system probably explains why he struggles to sleep eight hours a night, and remains perpetually irritable, but Trump's consumption of more than 4,000 cans of Diet Coke a year nevertheless represents one of his most significant contributions to the US economy.

Those external drops of water are the most nutritious part of the drink. *(Jesus Rodriguez)*

Donald Junior and Eric Trump

Donald John Trump Junior and **Eric Trump** are the two sons of President Donald Trump and his first wife, Ivana. They are indistinguishable.

They currently serve as trustees of the Trump Organization, with the day-to-day responsibility of not stuffing up the business their father spent a lifetime building (and bankrupting and rebuilding). However, as he has refused to relinquish his ownership and can suspend the trust at any time, it's clear that Trump's trust in his eldest sons is as limited as his body's battery energy.

The Trump business is in fact in rude health, with enthusiastic interest from wealthy businessmen seeking influence, problematic foreign regimes and dubious overseas business partners*.

Early life

The Trump scions were raised in New York City but formed a special bond with their Slovenian grandfather, Miloš Zelníček, who taught them to hunt, fish and generally slaughter living creatures. This has led to a lifelong interest in killing, and the Trumps now frequently go on hunting trips where they murder leopards, elephants, waterbucks and other inedible creatures. They then take macabre photos, because killing an elephant is so much more satisfying when you pose for a selfie with its bloody, lifeless tail.

---

* For instance, his partner in the Trump Hotel Baku in Azerbaijan, the former transportation minister, whose business may be a front for Iran, according to the *New Yorker*. Trump's business deals in Georgia, India, Indonesia, the Philippines and Brazil have also involved controversial business partners beyond Donald Trump himself.

It's widely believed that if alien hunting aficionados ever come to the planet Earth in search of sport, as depicted in the movie *Predator*, the Trumps will be among the first humans selected as targets.

Involvement in politics

The Trumplings spoke at the 2016 Republican National Convention, because their father didn't believe he could win and so hadn't bothered to organise a compelling roster of speakers, as evidenced by the participation of the widely hated entrepreneur Peter Thiel, Dana White from the UFC, a bandana-wearing redneck from reality television show *Duck Dynasty* and actor Scott Baio.

Despite Trump's promise to keep his business at arm's length from politics, Trump's eldest sons are also his most avid supporters on social media, where their habit of making things worse has clearly been inherited from their father.

Personal lives

While both young men are obviously disappointments to their father, they both take after him in some respects. Both married women with part-Eastern European heritage in a lavish ceremony at Mar-a-Lago. Eric Trump's eponymous charitable foundation has come under investigation by the New York State Attorney General's office. And Donald Trump Junior's divorce is now pending after accusations of infidelity.

Donald Junior proposed to his girlfriend, Vanessa, outside a New Jersey jewellery store, which gave him a $100,000 diamond ring in return for some paparazzi photos being taken out the front, a stunt condemned as tacky even by Donald Trump Senior. For his next marriage, Donald Junior won't pose for a free ring worth anything less than a million.

Both sons have also been parodied on *Saturday Night Live*, which depicts Eric as the stupid one. This is highly unfair because, as Donald Trump was quoted as saying in *Fire and Fury*, both sons were at the back of the room when God was handing out brains. They thought this was a compliment.

The Trump Organization's succession planning is the subject of much speculation—it's unclear which son will be second-in-charge after Ivanka.[*]

 Donald J. Trump
@realDonaldTrump

Both Donald Junior and Eric Trump are valuable members of the Trump Organization, as my lawyer says you can't divorce immediate family members other than wives. And they are so easy to tell apart! Just call Ivana and ask her.

Donald Trump

Donald John Trump, born 14 June 1946, is the 45th president of the United States, a joke originally made by *The Simpsons* in March 2000.[†]

---

[*] At this rate, probably Barron.

[†] *The Simpsons* writer Dan Greaney told *TV Guide* in 2016 that he pitched the idea as a 'warning to America', as a Trump presidency seemed 'consistent with the vision of America going insane'. The show's prediction that President Trump would be followed by President Lisa Simpson seems unlikely to come true, however.

He is the oldest, richest and least qualified person ever to assume the presidency, having had no prior experience in government, the military, or running companies that generate more wealth than leaving the money he inherited from his father in an indexed fund would have.*

In 2018, *Forbes* estimated that he was the 766th richest person in the world, with a net worth of 3.1 billion dollars, a figure that, were he not distracted by the presidency, would have caused him to sue, as he maintains the value of his brand alone is worth many billions.

Trump's platform has been described as populist, protectionist and nationalist, which is a polite way of saying it's quite racist.

His victory in the 2016 presidential election was a surprise for him, a crushing disappointment for his opponent, Hillary Clinton, and the greatest disaster imaginable for his wife, Melania.

Family

Trump's ancestors on his father Fred Trump's side hail from the German village of Kallstadt, where several generations of Drumpfs, as they were originally known, were famous throughout the Palatinate region for selling red felt Tyrolean hats embroidered with 'Macht Deutschland Wieder Groß'.

Trump's mother, Mary Anne, grew up on an island off Scotland, a heritage that would later be celebrated by her son Donald as he tried to strong-arm the Scottish government over a wind farm. Donald is fond of

---

* This was claimed by S.V. Dáte in an influential article for *National Review*, and has been affirmed by calculations provided in articles in *Vox* and other places. It may also be affirmed by reading all the entries in this book about the Trump businesses that lost money.

islands, having lived most of his life on Manhattan, although he is entirely indifferent to the rising sea levels that threaten to engulf them.

Fred and Mary Anne Trump had five children: Maryanne,* a future Federal Appeals Court judge; Fred Junior; Elizabeth; Donald, a future federal defendant; and Elizabeth.

Early life

Fred Trump was a wealthy property developer, and growing up with a butler and limousines formed the luxurious tastes of his young son. Interviews with his former classmates have revealed that Trump had a reputation as a playground bully handy with an insult and who would never admit he was wrong, which could have been guessed without going to the trouble of tracking old classmates down.

At the age of thirteen, Trump was abruptly sent to the New York Military Academy, after his parents discovered he frequently travelled into Manhattan without their permission, exploring Central Park and buying switchblades, reflecting his life-long interest in making cuts. His new boarding school was 70 miles away, and had a reputation for discipline: misbehaving students were smacked and forced to fight one another in a boxing ring, as WWE had not yet been invented. After leaving the school, Trump was determined never to be disciplined again.

Military school might have given Trump a lifelong respect for those who made the great sacrifice of military service, but instead bestowed a lifelong aversion to doing so himself. His greatest achievement at the Military

---

* Unlike her mother, she did not have a space in her name. Like her brother, she used to have a good relationship with the Clintons, one of whom appointed her to the federal bench.

Academy was replacing the light fitting in his dorm room with an ultraviolet globe to get a tan back in the days before he had ready access to pancake makeup*.

In 1964, Trump enrolled at Fordham University, New York City, but two years later transferred to the Wharton business school at the University of Pennsylvania, obtaining a Bachelor of Science in economics and lifetime bragging rights about going to a prestigious MBA school where he did not study for an MBA.

Trump did not fight in the Vietnam War, obtaining four student deferments during his university days, and then, on graduating in 1968, found himself eligible for military service. However, after a medical examination he was disqualified—due, his campaign would later claim, to bone spurs in both heels, which debilitating condition fortunately never prevented the young Trump from playing football and basketball at school.

Relationships

In 1977, Donald Trump married the Czech model Ivana Zelníčková in Manhattan. They had three children, Donald Junior (born 1977), Ivanka (born 1981) and Eric (born with a regrettably close resemblance to his father). In 1992, the couple divorced after Trump cheated on Ivana with Marla Maples, although his first wife may have been forewarned the marriage would not last when her husband reportedly told friends, 'I would never buy Ivana any decent jewels or pictures. Why give her negotiable assets?'†

---

* Paul Schwartzman and Michael Miller's profile in the *Washington Post* also says he considered going to film school in California after graduation, but instead he stayed in New York and became a big-budget production himself.

† *Vanity Fair* reported this in 1990—and their reportage on Trump is usually reliable, as they are the experts on vanity.

Trump's affair with Maples was far from private—in 1990, the front cover of the *New York Post* featured a full-page headline saying 'Marla Boasts To Her Pals About Donald—Best Sex I've Ever Had'. The story apparently came about after Trump called the *Post* demanding a front cover after a run of stories sympathetic to Ivana. When the editor had protested that cover stories were usually about murder, money or sex, Trump supplied the quote in the headline, which raises the question of whether Marla had ever had any other lovers with which to compare. When the editor demanded confirmation, former *Post* reporter Jill Brooke recounts that Trump asked Marla whether she'd said that, and she replied, 'Yes, Donald'. Maples now denies saying so, and claims it must have been someone else. Perhaps John Barron?

In October 1993, Marla Maples gave birth to Tiffany Trump, who was named after the jeweller adjacent to Trump Tower known for selling diamond solitaire rings. The name may have been a hint—Maples and Trump were married two months later. They divorced in 1999, and Tiffany grew up with her mother in California, as Trump's busy schedule of self-absorption has never allowed much time for childrearing.

In 2005, Trump married his third wife, Melania Knauss, at Mar-a-Lago. She had a son, Barron, the following year, while the boy's father allegedly had Stormy Daniels shortly afterwards.

Health

Trump is a teetotaller and non-smoker—his only vices are fast food and his personality. He apparently never uses illegal drugs either—although pharmacologists suggest, given his extreme exuberance, irritability and lack of social inhibitions, that his body apparently exudes some kind of natural cocaine.

The president is either in the very best of health, to judge by reports provided by his doctors, or dangerously obese, to judge by his appearance and lifestyle. During the campaign, his personal physician, Dr Harold Bornstein, released a letter describing Trump's condition as 'astonishingly excellent', and claiming that 'if elected, Mr Trump, I can state unequivocally, will be the healthiest individual ever elected to the presidency'. This would have been a contentious claim even for the buff, basketball-playing Barack Obama, let alone his successor. However, in 2018, Bornstein revealed that Trump had dictated the letter, which surprised everyone who had not read the letter. Trump later sacked Bornstein after he revealed that the president took the hair loss drug Propecia.

In early 2018, Trump's White House physician, Dr Ronny Jackson, who is also a naval rear admiral, released a report claiming that his boss was in 'excellent health', which could only be refuted by calculating his body mass index. Trump was certainly in much better health than Jackson's career was after Trump nominated him to run the Department of Veterans' Affairs: troubling revelations during the confirmation process meant that Jackson was ultimately forced to withdraw his application and resign as the president's physician. Dr Bornstein attests that Trump is the healthiest individual ever to destroy the life of a doctor whom he nominated to a Cabinet role for which he was patently unqualified.

In 2018, Jackson released the results of cognitive tests that President Trump had apparently asked him to perform, claiming that the president had no cognitive impairment whatsoever. These results were immediately contradicted by a more definitive daily indicator: the president's Twitter account.

Religion

Trump considers himself Presbyterian, following his mother's family tradition; however, he has said that he does not ask God for forgiveness because he hasn't done anything wrong. The Christian right takes a similar view.

Accolades

At the end of 2016, *Time* named him their person of the year; however Trump strenuously objected to the title 'President of the Divided States of America', thereby justifying it. *Forbes* named him the second most powerful person in the world—behind Vladimir Putin, which raised no objection from Trump.

In 2010, Robert Gordon University in Scotland awarded him an honorary Doctor of Business Administration, which it later revoked following the racist statements Trump made during his campaign, and because it was feared that he would use his honorary title to write himself bogus medical certificates.

Political affiliations

Donald Trump was a Democrat prior to 1987, when he made his first serious gesture towards running for the presidency. Spending nearly $100,000, he placed an advertisement in several major newspapers imploring America to stop paying for the military defence of countries that could afford to fund their own security. Making America a cheapskate again has remained a core belief ever since, consistent with his cherished business principle of renegotiating every bill he ever receives. Later in his political career, Trump also learned the value of inflammatory statements and publicity stunts, and hasn't needed to pay for an ad since.

In 1999, Trump established an exploratory committee to seek the nomination of the Reform Party, the independent party founded by Ross Perot. A poll matching him against eventual nominees George W. Bush and Al Gore put him at 7 per cent. This contradicted his frequently stated and mocked belief that he could win, and he pulled out.

Presumably concluding that trying to run as a major party candidate was a more sensible approach to getting elected, Trump returned to the Democratic Party in 2001, publicly pondered running in 2004, and then in 2008 endorsed Republican John McCain for president even though he'd been captured, unlike his opponent, Barack Obama. After McCain's defeat, Trump changed his registration to Republican, which naturally was a reflection of his rapidly evolving political views rather than rank opportunism.

In 2011, Trump speculated about running for president as part of his extensive Birtherism Media Tour—some polls placed him ahead of the ultimate GOP nominee, Mitt Romney, and suggested he'd have a chance against Obama. That year he was mocked by the president at the White House Correspondents' Dinner, leading both to an increased desire to run and an increased reluctance to do so. Trump finally announced that he wouldn't be running but that he definitely would have won if he had, which at the time seemed even funnier than any of Obama's widely acclaimed witticisms.

Obama's successful raid on Osama bin Laden, which took place the same night as the dinner, probably also influenced Trump's decision, both because it significantly increased Obama's approval ratings and because it illustrated that the president was more ruthless about dispatching opposition than he had previously indicated.

Trump was perceived as a blowhard who had chickened out, and many thought his talk about running for office was a publicity stunt for *The Apprentice*. But Trump would soon reveal himself to be a blowhard who would not chicken out the next time, and ultimately succeeded in becoming a blowhard president.

Presidential campaign, 2015–2016

In 2015, Donald Trump surprised many by moving beyond his traditional pretence at running, joining the most crowded presidential primary field in history. In June that year, he launched his campaign the way he would ultimately spend so much of his presidency—cross-promoting a Trump property, and making easily disproven boasts about the size of his audience, beginning his remarks by saying, 'There's been no crowd like this.' But after descending his own golden escalators to begin his press conference, he also irrevocably lowered the tone of the Republican primaries, saying, 'When Mexico sends its people, they're not sending their best. They're sending people that have lots of problems . . . They're bringing drugs, they're bringing crime. They're rapists.' Showing early form for his remarks after Charlottesville, however, he then added, 'And some, I assume, are good people.'

These remarks led NBC to sever its ties with the new candidate. It was only the beginning of a campaign plagued with controversy, as the tape of Trump's boasts about genitalia-grabbing sexual assault surfaced, and he was investigated for possible collusion with Russia and obstruction of justice. But some Trumps, we assume, are good people.

It took Trump the better part of a year to overcome Ted Cruz and John Kasich and the fifteen other major candidates and make the transition from presumptuous candidate to presumptive nominee. He won the nomination with a little over 14 million votes, an all-time record. It was the last popular vote he would win.

Early in his campaign against Hillary Clinton, his opponent had a commanding lead in the polls until the FBI announced it was reopening its investigation into her email server—in other words, Trump's campaign received an email bounce.

Trump and Clinton appeared in three especially brutal debates, during which Trump walked into Clinton's shot while she was speaking, invited women who had accused Bill Clinton of impropriety as a means of defusing his own *Access Hollywood* controversy, and threatened to refuse to accept the outcome of the election.

Donald Trump and one of his many white male fans. *(Ali Shaker/VOA)*

A school photo—the closest Trump would come to serving in uniform. *(Seth Poppel/Yearbook Library)*

As ever, the volley of criticism directed against Trump for these things failed to hurt his popularity, and may even have bolstered it.

On election day, Trump lost to Hillary Clinton by 46.1 per cent to 48.2 per cent, or nearly three million votes. And yet, because in their wisdom the Founding Fathers decided to implement a system that's best described as 'undemocratic', 'terrible', and 'Why does everyone venerate the Founding Fathers when they came up with this dreadful mess?', Trump became president thanks to an electoral college victory of an overwhelming 304 to 227. *(See* **Electoral college***)*

Within hours of assuming the presidency, Trump filed with the FEC to run in 2020, which means we're going to have to go through all this again.

Electoral college

In an electoral system like America's that allows voters to directly choose between several candidates for president, the votes could simply be totalled to give a 100 per cent accurate reflection of the will of the American people, ensuring the election is won by the person most voters think should be president.

The **electoral college** exists so that, regularly, this does not happen and a candidate most American voters think is a dangerous idiot gets elected instead, as happened in 1876, 1888, 2000 and 2016. In this way, the electoral college is unlike most colleges, in that marks do not necessarily influence the overall result.

Almost nobody without a political science degree understands how the electoral college works, which is a pity because the system has many interesting quirks. Each state is given the number of seats equal to the size of its congressional delegation—that is, the number of seats in both the House and the Senate. Consequently, tiny states like Vermont, Wyoming and the Dakotas, which only merit one seat in the population-based House of Representatives, get three seats in the 538-person electoral college because every state gets two senators.

Consequently voters in Wyoming, which has fewer than a million residents, enjoy four times the electoral college representation that Californian voters do.

In most states, the winner takes all the delegates, so a candidate can get 50.01 per cent of the vote and 100 per cent of the electoral college seats. In other states, the seats are split proportionally. These differences appeal to Americans, who generally believe there should be a range of systems used across the states—some good and some stupid—rather than all of them using the fairest system possible.

The electoral college is, unnecessarily and archaically, still composed of 538 actual people who convene in each state capital to vote a few days after election day, even though the next president is already known shortly after everyone finishes voting. These electors are prohibited from gathering in one location because of the chance of collusion and because America is weird about theoretical central government oppression.

Many members of the electoral college aren't bound to vote the way their state did, and can instead become 'faithless electors' and cast their presidential vote however they want, which is definitely a sensible, democratic approach to conducting elections in a nation of 320 million people.

The first president to win the electoral college vote but lose the popular vote was Andrew Jackson—which is perhaps why, as a fellow loser, he's Trump's political hero. It's also possible that, because of this parallel, he's the only historical president Trump has heard of.

The electoral college exists because of the fears of Southern politicians that if they didn't get proportionally more votes than they deserved on the basis of their smaller populations, they might lose political power and have to relinquish slavery. This is a useful indicator of how relevant and worthwhile this system remains today.

In the 2016 election, Hillary Clinton lost the electoral college vote by 227 to Donald Trump's 304 despite winning nearly three million more votes. That the electoral college was capable of electing Donald Trump is an entirely sufficient reason to abandon it.

Empire State Building

The **Empire State Building** is the most famous skyscraper in New York, and perhaps the world. Donald Trump once paid nothing for half of it, as one might expect from the legend behind *The Art of the Deal*, but he ultimately had to give up his stake, as one might expect given the patchier reality of Donald Trump's businesses.

History

In 1994, Trump was given a half share in the building by its Japanese owner, who had paid $42 million for it in 1991 and given it to his daughter, Kiko Nakahara, to run. She had decided that the best way to make money from their ownership would be to evict the current master leaseholders, who had occupation rights to the building until 2075—which was why buying the building itself was relatively cheap, given the lack of flexibility. Nakahara figured the best way to seize control would be to get NYC property whiz Donald Trump to find a way to have the lease invalidated in return for an equal share in the building's ownership. At this time Trump was in severe financial difficulty thanks to problems with his casino empire, so the price of $0 was right.

Trump immediately devised an ambitious plan to convert the building into expensive condos, even though he had many legal hurdles to pass first, and planted stories in the city's major newspaper that claimed, with great fanfare, he had bought the building.

Takeover attempt

The following year, Trump sued the leaseholders over the state of the building, saying it was a 'high-rise slum' overrun by mice, with slow elevators and dark hallways—but he lost both the case and the subsequent appeal. Then his Japanese business partners got into unrelated legal troubles of their own. In the end, Trump sold his share to the leaseholders, making a profit compared with his initial zero outlay.

Trump's attempt to purchase the building and turn it into condos trading under the name 'Trump Empire State Building Apartments' is considered the most troubling assault on the New York landmark since King Kong.

Environmental Protection Agency

Usually the **Environmental Protection Agency** (EPA) is the federal body tasked with the conservation of the planet, but under its Trump-appointed administrator, Scott Pruitt, the EPA's new understanding of 'protection' was that the environment had better look out, or else it'll get whacked, *capiche?*

As attorney general of Oklahoma, Pruitt took a stand against what he termed the 'activist' nature of the EPA—that is, the

Pruitt in a more friendly environment. *(Gage Skidmore)*

part that acts to achieve its objectives. He sued the organisation fourteen times during Obama's presidency in a bid to prevent it passing laws to safeguard clean air and water, because apparently fighting nationwide environmental regulations was a huge priority for Oklahoma's top legal officer.

This campaign reflected Pruitt's personal conviction that climate change is a hoax perpetrated by 99 per cent of scientists but easily disproven by the ornery common sense of one plucky, deeply religious lawyer from Oklahoma with no scientific expertise, but a deep suspicion of all things scientific dating back to the scam known as evolution.

Pruitt had been assisted in his battles against the EPA by not only his deep personal faith in God, but also the deep pockets of oil companies, who answered his prayers by funding his campaigns and helpfully suggesting which EPA regulations to challenge, and even the wording to use. With their help, Pruitt attempted to argue that there is no evidence that carbon dioxide emissions cause climate change, and that warming is caused by humans, if the 'climate' is even 'changing' in the first place.

While a grand total of none of Pruitt's lawsuits against the EPA have been successful so far, his long struggle against Barack Obama's administration was all that Donald Trump needed to hear to be convinced that Pruitt was the perfect man to run the EPA, in the sense of run it into the ground.

Besides his climate battles, Pruitt's only significant prior interest in environmentalism was his support for a critically endangered species, Jeb Bush, before his hopes of a third Bush presidency became entirely extinct. However, Trump was able to overlook this, given the pair's common enemies—Barack Obama, the EPA itself, and science in general.

As EPA administrator, Pruitt successfully shrunk the agency's reach and begun winding back Obama's climate regulations. However, many of his reforms failed to survive legal challenges, leading to the situation in which the courts were protecting the environment from the Environmental Protection Agency.

President Trump ordered Pruitt to cut the agency's expenditure by 24 per cent, but Pruitt took the initiative to divert even more funds away from the environment by wasting them. To this end, he regularly travelled first class or on a chartered flight, unlike his predecessors, and even used military aircraft when commercial flights were readily available, racking up hundreds of thousands of dollars in unnecessary travel expenses. If the courts wouldn't let him roll back clean air regulations, Pruitt was determined to pollute the atmosphere himself, one flight at a time.

Pruitt also expanded his security detail to an unprecedented eighteen people, because members of the public were occasionally known to berate him for what he was doing to the environment. He also spent $43,000 building a soundproof booth in his office, even though there was already a secure phone in place, as he was paranoid that his EPA co-workers were trying to undermine him. Pruitt may have been correct about this—although clearly he started it. As wasteful as the expenditure may seem, however, the notion of Pruitt sitting in a soundproof box seemed the perfect symbol for his approach to running the Environmental Protection Authority.

Pruitt was also trying to negotiate a controversy resulting from his decision to spend hundreds of thousands of dollars on a trip to Morocco—comprising one workday and a two-night stopover in Paris—for the stated purpose of promoting US liquid natural gas exports, which has not previously been considered an essential part of the agency's environment protection mission.

Coincidentally, when he made this trip, Pruitt was living in a Washington DC condominium owned by a lobbyist whose firm is the only US exporter of natural gas. It has been claimed that he paid a mere $50 per night to stay in the luxurious Capitol Hill condo, and that his daughter also received free accommodation.

This delightful mutually beneficial arrangement led even some Republican members of Congress to call for his resignation—perhaps the clearest instance of Pruitt's only successful conservation effort: the continued existence of the 'swamp' of lobbyist power networks that President Trump had promised to drain.

Noting a frosty change in his work climate, Pruitt resigned on 6 July 2018. He was replaced by his deputy Andrew Wheeler, a former coal lobbyist, who was nevertheless welcomed by many EPA staffers because of his reputation for being not paranoid, not corrupt and passably competent. Pruitt's tenure will be outlived, however, by several investigations into it.

It is not yet clear whether Wheeler will be confirmed in the role, as some senators have pointed out that it might be prudent for the EPA to be led by someone with an interest in environmental protection.

Pruitt's departure was perhaps most welcomed by the staff of the White House Mess, where Pruitt frequently lingered just in case the president called. He apparently lunched there so often that the White House asked him to visit less frequently. His exit also benefits one Washington lobbyist, who can now charge the market rate for his spare room.

Fake news

Fake news, also known as 'clickbait', 'propaganda', 'satire', 'lies' or 'verifiable truth', depending on the context, is a media report that is either deliberately untrue, or that the subject of the report asserts is untrue, would like to be untrue, or simply claims is untrue so that they no longer have to deal with it.

The term has transitioned from describing false news stories designed to appeal to a reader's prejudices so that they share them online, generating profitable advertising revenue for the publisher, to a catch-all rebuttal to any meticulously researched story published by the world's most reputable news organisations.

The first recorded use of fake news was by Ramses the Great, the thirteenth-century Egyptian pharaoh who ordered images of himself and his army defeating the Hittites to be featured on the walls of his temples, although historians believe that the Battle of Kadesh was in fact a draw. Much of the fake news produced today is also about getting hits.

According to Donald J. Trump, however, the term was invented by Donald J. Trump. In an interview with Mike Huckabee, he said, 'The media is really, the word, one of the greatest of all the terms I've come up with, is "fake".' So even his claim to have invented fake news is fake news, although not in the Trumpian sense.

Except he really did say this, meaning that it's not fake news. Except that Trump will probably later claim that him saying he invented fake news was *itself* fake news. Herein lies the problem with the phrase's complex evolution, and the extent to which its original meaning has been inverted—and also why we should all just stop using it.

Nevertheless, at the moment it is entirely true that Donald Trump tweeting a story is 'fake news' is entirely sufficient repudiation of it, at least in his supporters' minds, and will inoculate him from any consequences.

Usage during 2016 election

Macedonia's 'fake news' mills

During the 2016 presidential campaign, many of the fabricated stories favouring Donald J. Trump emanated from Veles, Macedonia, where a host of teenagers concocted articles designed to appeal to the most credulous section of the US electorate: Trump voters. Investigative reporters identified over one hundred websites publishing invented political news in the small city. Their claims, included that Hillary Clinton was being indicted for her email security breach, that she had said in 2013 people like Trump should run for president because he couldn't be bought, that Pope Francis had endorsed Trump, and, perhaps most plausibly, that a sex tape of Bill Clinton had just been leaked.

Hillary Clinton was also accused of being involved with a child sex ring connected with a pizza shop in Washington DC, which was not a real crime—as opposed to the one committed by a guillible reader whom the article inspired to take an assault rifle to the Comet Ping Pong pizzeria and open fire. Fortunately, nobody was hurt, although an innocent ping pong table took a bullet. The young fake news entrepreneurs of Veles weren't motivated by support for the Republican cause, but rather the huge advertising revenue to be made when the links were shared on Facebook. In a sense, however, the desire to make large amounts of money while ignoring questions of morality made them natural allies of Donald J. Trump, who has given his name to at least one pyramid scheme besides his 2016 campaign. *(See also* **Trump Network**.*)*

Indeed, Trump has long had a beneficial connection with Eastern Europe, which, before it began supplying many of his votes, also supplied many of his wives.

Paul Horner

Another influential producer of fake news was the late Arizonan comedian and provocateur Paul Horner, a prolific writer whose work was either satirical or deliberately deceptive, depending on one's opinion of his intentions. He had previously come to prominence by claiming that Barack Obama had personally paid for a Muslim museum to stay open during a government shutdown, which was repeated by Fox News, and had on several occasions 'revealed' that Banksy's real name was Paul Horner.

During the 2016 campaign, Horner's webpages were shared by campaign assets like Corey Lewandowski and family liabilities like Eric Trump. Horner claimed that he wanted Trump supporters to 'look like idiots for sharing my stories', but since the election many commentators, including

Horner himself, concluded that as he helped put a man he despised in the White House, it's unclear who the idiot in the equation ultimately turned out to be.

Russia

Many of these articles were widely shared by Russian social-media trolls using fake accounts created in order to game algorithms and give the false impression of popular support. This sophisticated, systematic organisation could be considered evidence of the Putin regime's documented assistance to the Trump campaign, had Trump not described any such link between his victory and Russia as 'fake news', thus entirely alleviating everyone's concerns.

'Fake news' claims by President Trump

In the months after his election, the president increasingly took to describing media outlets as fake, especially CNN. In January 2018, that network published an article calculating that Trump called news organisations and their stories fake at least once a day, a claim Trump supporters presumably rejected as fake. Some other things he has dismissed as fake include:

- the Russia dossier, the intelligence memo alleging collaboration between Trump's campaign and the Russian government,
- Michael Wolff's exposé *Fire and Fury: Inside the Trump White House*,
- all of CNN, NBC, ABC, CBS, the *Washington Post* and *The New York Times*,
- the 'FAKE NEWS media' generally,
- the claim that Steve Bannon was running the White House (which has been vindicated as fake news, because clearly nobody was),

Around the world

Trump's phrase has been eagerly adopted by autocrats everywhere as a means of denying plausible accusations of human rights violations. Among those deploying the charge of 'fake news' have been Syrian president Bashar al-Assad while disputing an Amnesty report about state-sanctioned killings, the Chinese government in denying torturing an activist, and Australia's own minister for home affairs, Peter Dutton, in rebutting claims a boatload of asylum seekers was being detained in Darwin.

 Donald J. Trump
@realDonaldTrump

I in fact invented 'Fake' long before 2016. Ask any student who went to Trump University!

Fake News Awards

The Fake News Trophy, later The Most Dishonest And Corrupt Media Awards Of The Year, and finally the **Fake News Awards**[*] was an event created by Donald Trump to combine his two favourite things: showbiz and complaining about the media.

Trump initially conceived the event in a tweet in November 2017, when he wrote, 'We should have a contest as to which of the Networks, plus CNN and not including Fox, is the most dishonest, corrupt and/or distorted in its political coverage of your favorite President (me).'

---

[*] Nicknamed 'Fakies' by some on social media, who perhaps treated the awards with less than the respect due to an initiative of the president of the United States.

While this first seemed like a joke—or at least as close as Trump gets to a joke, which is a whinge about how unfairly he's treated—the White House proceeded to make preparations for the event, and his campaign emailed supporters in December, asking them to compare the fakeness of various news stories.

The awards were scheduled for 8 January, amid speculation that Trump was planning a gala live event, and then deferred, which heightened suspicions that either Trump had something big planned to get revenge on the dastardly perpetrators of fake news, or that he had no idea what the event was going to be and wanted to buy more time.

Final awards process

In the end, the latter explanation seems likely, as the awards disappointed in several respects. Firstly, the winners were predominantly journalists or outlets that had undeniably done something wrong and apologised, issued a correction or even sacked those involved in a genuine error. Those looking to be entertained by Trump's extravagant media-bashing found very little to enjoy, even as his perennial punching bag CNN scooped the pool with four awards, followed by the 'failing' *New York Times* with two.

The second frustration was that instead of a gala live ceremony in the tradition of other awards nights, as had been hoped for by ironic fans of the concept, the 'event' merely consisted of a page posted on the Republican National Committee website, under the title 'The Highly Anticipated 2017 Fake News Awards'.

This meant that the awards ultimately lacked even the official imprimatur of the White House—appropriate, admittedly, for such a self-indulgent exercise, but still something of a let-down for those hoping to be amused by Trump's latest outlandish exercise in animosity.

Most frustratingly of all, the enormous interest in the results broke the RNC website, which, to add irony to injury, displayed an error message saying, 'We're making it great again'. Eventually, early visitors who had successfully connected to the site shared the results on social media, and as the disappointing realisation that the awards were straighter than anticipated spread among earnest and sarcastic fans alike, traffic quickly dissipated.

The surprising credibility of the awards led many to suspect that the whole endeavour had been dramatically circumscribed by John Kelly, except perhaps for the one bonus category slamming any organisation that had reported on the links between Russia and the Trump campaign, which was referred to as 'perhaps the greatest hoax ever perpetrated on the American people'.

The ironic campaigning for awards by late-night comedy shows may also have encouraged the White House to reduce their scope. *The Daily Show* took out an ad in *The New York Times*, while *The Late Show* host Stephen Colbert bought a billboard in Times Square, parodying the 'For Your Consideration' ads that studios take out before the Oscars.

However, it's hoped that with Kelly's sidelining in 2018, the awards will return as a far grander affair, ideally a gala live broadcast from Mar-a-Lago hosted by Sean Hannity.

Family separation policy

As part of its 'zero tolerance' of illegal immigrants, and immigrants in general, the Trump administration began separating children from their accompanying parents or other adults when they were apprehended crossing the border, even when legally applying for asylum. More than 2300 children were detained under the programme, and some of them were kept in wire mesh cages and allegedly forcibly given medication.

Attorney General Jeff Sessions claimed that the policy was justified in the Bible, which in Romans 13 charges believers to follow any laws of a government—a provision which was formerly used to defend slavery and could hypothetically be used to argue for genocide.

Homeland Security Secretary Kirstjen Nielsen first denied it occurring, tweeting 'We do not have a policy of separating families at the border. Period.' Then she insisted it was demanded by federal law, which it wasn't,

Immigrant children receiving a helpful lesson from the United States Government about why the caged bird sings. *(US Government)*

and then called on Congress to change the law, despite Congress being run by her own party. She subsequently defended the policy and argued that many of the minors detained were only posing as a fake family unit, which still wouldn't explain why they should have been detained for being exploited by the adults accompanying them. Nielsen also called the suggestion that the separations were being used as a bargaining chip to get the border wall built 'offensive', even though Trump and his press secretary had both explicitly said this.

For his part, President Trump said that he '[hated] to see the children being taken away', and that it was a 'horrible law' for which the Democrats were responsible, even though there was no law requiring such a separation, and the Democrats were as far from being in government as possible under the American system.

Relaxation

After much criticism, the president abandoned the separation policy, in a rare example of him softening his extremely harsh stance on immigration in response to an outcry from the public, the media, or most likely Ivanka.

A court subsequently issued an injunction suspending the policy, but not before Trump held a ceremony where he issued an executive order, with much fanfare, in order to reverse a policy that hadn't been created by an executive order in the first place.

It's understood that Trump was surprised by the backlash to the policy, as his own approach to parenting has been to separate himself from his children as much as possible, leaving their mothers to raise them.

Fashion and Donald Trump

The president has been a trendsetter for years, and continues to be hugely influential in **fashion**, even from within the Oval Office. Admittedly, it's in the arena of what not to do, but he plays a significant role nonetheless.*

Makeup

The president wears pancake television makeup each day, just as he did on *The Apprentice*, but unlike NBC's skilled makeup artists, he is unable to get the foundation close to his eyes, or achieve a tone that would help him resemble an ordinary human being. Consequently, his current skin hue is somewhere between 'solarium overdose', 'Fanta' and 'Oompa-Loompa with eyeholes'.

Red tie

Though Trump's trademark comically oversized red tie has its critics, some menswear experts have hailed it as a broad red stroke of genius, pointing out it minimises his gut by causing the eye to marvel instead at the vast extent of necktie. Trump's habit of attaching the short end to the long section with sticky tape has led to fashionable men everywhere simply abandoning neckties altogether.

---

* While reflecting on the personal appearance of a politician is usually crass and inappropriate, Donald Trump should be an exception because he has spent so much time making disparaging comments about women's appearances. In the interests of balance, however, he rated Ivanka a ten.

Suiting

While master tailors have traditionally followed the contours of the body, emphasising the customer's flattering features and de-emphasising their shortcomings, Trump's habiliment represents nothing less than a completely new approach to gentlemen's suiting. He begins with a suit perfectly sized for his tall yet rotund body, and then exchanges it for one three or four sizes larger. The resulting suit swims around his figure with the sort of loose flow that is usually only to be found in a kimono, or a ladies' evening gown. Though past presidents of the United States have had a notable influence on menswear fashion, such as JFK's preference for two-button, single-breasted suiting, Trump's style has yet to catch on.

Sportswear

The president is an avid golfer, and is often photographed on the links, with each image of the president in white sportswear leading to the same inexorable conclusion applicable to all men of Trump's age and physique: don't be photographed on the links.

Hairstyle

The important thing to note about the president's hair is that it is his own. It may be dyed a shade of blonde that occurs nowhere in nature, it may be augmented by the Propecia that Trump sacked his doctor for disclosing he used, and the careful arrangement of what remains may be swept into an elaborate comb-over that resembles nothing so much as soft-serve ice-cream, but it's absolutely, unquestionably, his own hair.

When Trump steps into the wind, the advanced progression of his male pattern baldness is rendered only too obvious as the surviving strands get blown straight up into the air. Any gentleman suffering from the early stages of hair loss will find even a cursory examination of the remarkable construction that is Donald Trump's hair an irrefutable argument for a buzz cut.

Trump Foundation

While most wealthy people establish charitable foundations in order to give their own money to worthy causes, the **Donald J. Trump Foundation** has in recent years been used to funnel other people's money into making Donald Trump look generous, as well as providing other benefits for his family, his businesses and the man himself. After a two-year investigation, the state of New York is suing the foundation for self-dealing, violating campaign finance laws, and improper co-ordination with Trump's presidential campaign, meaning that one of its major beneficiaries in the years ahead will be lawyers. After winning the election, Trump announced his intention to dissolve the foundation to avoid 'even the appearance of any conflicts' with his new role, meaning that although Trump has refused to divest his for-profit business, he's happy to shut down the part of his operation that was, at least notionally, intended to help others.

The foundation's dissolution was delayed, however, by the need for the New York State attorney general to finish up its investigation of it.

Controversies

The Donald J. Trump Foundation was established in 1988 to distribute the profits of his book *Trump: The Art of the Deal*. Trump has contributed at least $5.5 million to his eponymous foundation, but since he contributed

$35,000 in 2008, the donations have come from other, non-personal sources. One example being investigated is the donation of $5 million by Vince and Linda McMahon of the WWE after Trump's appearances at Wrestlemania. Investigators are querying whether the foundation has been given personal income due to Trump so as to avoid taxes.

Investigations by the *Washington Post* and others have found that many of the charitable donations that Trump claimed to have made personally were in fact made by his foundation using money donated by others.

Trump's foundation is alleged to have:

- delayed part of a $6 million donation to veterans' charities. While Trump claimed to have donated $1,000,000 of his personal money at a fundraiser in April 2016, he admitted in May 2016 that he had only done so the following week after media criticism
- failed to make the donations to the victims of 9/11 that were promised during an appearance on *The Howard Stern Show*
- made grants to the National Museum of Catholic Art and Library, whose chairman was also head of the Building and Construction Trades Council of Greater New York
- used Trump Foundation grants to further his political career despite the prohibition on charities engaging in politics
- used foundation money to settle Trump Organization lawsuits, including a $100,000 donation to a veteran's charity after the Trump Organization was sued over an excessively large flagpole at Mar-a-Lago
- purchased multiple portraits of Trump, which were then exhibited in the public areas of his venues
- bought footballer Tim Tebow's helmet, the whereabouts of which is currently unknown, (and the point of which is also currently unknown).

Washington Post journalist David Fahrenthold* contacted more than four hundred charities that Trump claimed he had donated to. Fahrenthold's investigation found that Trump had made only one personal donation between January 2009 and 23 May 2016: to the Police Athletic League. It was less than $10,000—and may have been an accounting error.

Of course, the precise extent of Donald Trump's personal charitable donations cannot be determined, because he hasn't released his personal tax returns.

Fox & Friends

Fox & Friends is a morning television program that airs on the US Fox News channel seven days a week. It describes itself as fair and balanced, which is to say it's profoundly right of centre.

More casual, friendly and couch-based than Fox's other daily programming, *Fox & Friends* has always involved two white men, and one white woman for diversity, and tends to steer away from the wall-to-wall fury that features in the network's prime-time slots, opting instead for furious agreement.

President Trump's early morning tweets so frequently echo comments made on *Fox & Friends* that it's widely assumed co-hosts Steve Doocy, Brian Kilmeade and Ainsley Earhardt are the only friends he has.

---

* Fahrenthold won the Pulitzer Prize for his investigation into Trump's foundation and personal donations, making him the only person to get anything out of Trump's many promises of donations.

Donald J. Trump ✅
@realDonaldTrump

Fox & Friends is the best Show and often says what I am thinking before I think it. Like all my many friends, they are welcome at Mar-a-Lago if they pay the $200,000 joining fee!

Goldman Sachs

During the 2016 campaign, Donald Trump said that the powerful investment bank **Goldman Sachs** had 'total control' over both Hillary Clinton and Ted Cruz, and criticised Clinton for her well-paid speeches to merchant banks. It was perhaps unsurprising that Trump was so critical of Goldmans, as it had long refused to take him on as a client.

The bank contributed so many alumni to recent Republican and Democratic administrations alike that it earned the nickname Government Sachs. Given Trump's intention that his administration 'drain the swamp', to use his phrase, he was determined to recruit no one whatsoever from Goldman Sachs.

No one, that is, except Treasury Secretary Steven Mnuchin, National Economic Council Director Gary Cohn, Deputy National Security Advisor Dina Powell, Director of Communications Anthony Scaramucci and Chief White House Strategist Steve Bannon.

Then again, most of the Goldman alumni that Trump immediately recruited on taking office have already departed the West Wing, and largely returned to working for organisations run with a modicum of professionalism—in

Powell's case, Goldman Sachs. In that sense, Trump has successfully drained the swamp of the people he himself hired.

Trump Golf

The dignified and respectable sport of **golf** is the ideal pursuit for Donald J. Trump. It combines his passion for hitting things with his desire to avoid physical exercise—except for moments spent standing with club in hand, players travel seated in a buggy and run down its electric battery rather than their non-rechargeable body batteries (*see also* **Battery theory**). On one recent excursion, Trump broke golf protocol by driving his buggy onto the green.

By frequently playing golf, Trump is also able to maintain the most fundamental rule he has about his leisure time: that he should never leave a Trump property.

Trump first began constructing golf courses in 1999, and now owns seventeen courses around the world, providing interested rich people in several countries with the opportunity to pay emoluments to the sitting president of the United States.

So far, President Trump has managed to fit in a game every five days, on average—which sounds like a lot, but even so, his time spent playing is tiny compared with the time he previously spent criticising Barack Obama for playing golf while president.

Some of Trump's most notable golf properties, tax minimisation schemes and lawsuits are outlined below.

Trump International Golf Club, West Palm Beach

Trump's first golf club sits near Mar-a-Lago on a parcel of land he was able to gain through the traditional Trump method: a lawsuit, in this case to stop planes flying across the oceanfront property he would later fly across in Air Force One. In a 2007 interview, he boasted that the county spent almost as much building him a freeway exit as he paid for the property, and casually noted that it costs $350,000 to join.

Trump National Golf Club, Bedminster, New Jersey

This property, a short distance from New York City, was part of the estate of car manufacturer John DeLorean, another entrepreneur who had a treasured business end up in bankruptcy. Trump managed to have the course classified as farmland, and consequently uses part of the land for growing hay and running eight goats. According to the *Wall Street Journal*, this reduced his tax bill from $80,000 to less than $1000. Visitors to the farm may be disappointed to find it sandwiched amid 36 golf fairways. Trump's attempt to rezone Trump Tower as farmland has been less successful.

The club, one of his most luxurious, also hosted one of the saddest occasions in Donald Trump's life—the wedding of his daughter Ivanka to Jared Kushner.

Trump National Golf Club, Jupiter, Florida

Trump bought this club, a former Ritz-Carlton, for $5 million, and had to pay the same amount again when he was sued by its former members after they attempted to cancel their memberships.

Trump National Golf Club, Los Angeles

Unusually for a Trump golf establishment, his LA course is open to the public, although as a round costs $300, it isn't really open to them. The oceanfront course had just been completed when the eighteenth hole slid into the sea, and Trump bought it for a song. Once the rectification work had been completed, it was the most expensive course ever constructed, at a total outlay of $264 million—which did not stop the Trump Organization from claiming to the LA County tax assessor that it was worth $10 million.

In 2008, Trump sued the city of Rancho Palos Verdes for $100 million, arguing that it had prevented him from improving the course to a standard consistent with the Trump image, which presumably means he was unable to ruin its stunning natural beauty with further development. The case was ultimately settled.

In 2015, the course was to host the PGA Grand Slam of Golf, but it was cancelled after Trump's comments about immigrants devalued the Trump image.

Trump National Golf Club, Washington, D.C.

Trump financed this purchase with a loan from the Chevy Chase Bank, which is genuinely a thing. The project attracted controversy because Trump removed hundreds of trees to provide a better view of the Potomac River—or, as his officials put it, because they were diseased and would cause soil erosion.

Trump added a plaque stating that 'many great American soldiers, both of the North and the South,* died at this spot. The casualties were so

---

* There were very fine people on both sides, apparently.

great that the water would turn red.' However, no Civil War battle took place there, meaning that in this case, the final casualty of war was truth.

Trump National Golf Club, Philadelphia

Trump couldn't resist buying a course that was 6,969 yards long.

Trump National Golf Club, Westchester, New York

When renovating this course, Trump's workers made unauthorised changes to its drainage system to improve its appearance and play. These alterations raised the water table by six feet, leading to the nearby town library, playing fields and swimming pool flooding in the next major storm.

During the 2016 election campaign, Hillary Clinton revealed that Trump and his representatives had pressured the club's architect to reduce his $140,000 bill to $50,000, and then only $25,000, and argued that Trump was bad for small business. As with the rest of what was said by the Clinton campaign, nobody cared.

During the campaign, it was also reported that the club featured a six-foot portrait of Trump, bought for $200,000 paid by the Donald J. Trump Foundation. Melania Trump had planned to hang it in the boardroom of the club, which only counts as a charitable purpose if you consider the opportunity to marvel at a huge picture of Trump a gift.

Trump International Golf Links, Scotland

Trump's first foothold in the traditional home of golf, north of Aberdeen in the United Kingdom, was purchased in 2006, and the Trump Organization intended to build a golf course capable of hosting a major tournament. But Trump's proposal was strongly opposed by many, including environmentalists who wanted to preserve historic sand dunes, and locals who at one point appeared to be facing compulsory purchase of their properties.

Likewise, a proposal to build an offshore wind farm was met with firm opposition from Trump, who called the turbines ugly. Trump went so far as to write to the first minister of Scotland, claiming that he was trying to act not just for the sake of his business interests but for the people of Scotland, citing his Scottish ancestry. He advised the minister that, should the wind farm go ahead, 'Your country will become a Third World wasteland that global investors will avoid.'

The first minister disagreed, and Trump's lawsuit ultimately failed in the Supreme Court in 2015. In April 2018, the world's most powerful wind turbine, with a 164-metre-high rotor, opened at the site, as part of Scotland's commitment to producing 100 per cent of its electricity via renewable energy by 2020. The experience made Trump all the more determined to ensure the United States produces none of its energy from renewables.

Trump Turnberry, Scotland

Despite Trump's threat to withdraw his business if the wind farm wasn't abandoned, he purchased a second, larger golf complex in the 'Third World wasteland' of Scotland in 2014. Turnberry in Ayrshire dates back to 1906, and is one of the legendary courses of British golf. It was the scene of the famous 'Duel in the Sun' between Jack Nicklaus and Tom Watson in 1977, so named because it was so unusual for any place in Scotland to experience sun.

Turnberry has hosted many Open Championships, one of the world's most prestigious tournaments. However, in 2015, the tournament's governing body announced that the 2020 tournament would no longer be played at Turnberry because of the controversial remarks Donald Trump made in launching his campaign for the presidency, indicating that his mind was too closed to host the Open.

Trump International Golf Links and Hotel, Ireland

The former Doonbeg Golf Club was bought by Donald Trump in 2014. The management applied to build a 2.8-kilometre-long sea wall to protect the property from 'global warming and its effect', even though Trump himself does not believe that global warming exists.

The move was opposed by environmentalists not on the grounds of abject hypocrisy, but because, ironically, it would have a detrimental impact on

Trump indulges in a round of golf and personal business promotion with the president of Japan, Shinzō Abe. *(Donald Trump/Twitter)*

the site's protected natural environment. Ultimately, two smaller barriers were built. These are the only walls that Donald Trump has recently been able to build.

Hope Hicks

White House director of strategic communications, 20 January 2017–12 September 2017

White House director of communications, 12 September 2017–29 March 2018

A long-time Trump aide who moved into the West Wing after the campaign, **Hope Hicks** was appointed communications director after Anthony Scaramucci, and quickly restored a degree of calm to that office by virtue of not being Anthony Scaramucci.

Hicks had previously been director of strategic communications, a position created by Donald Trump and the function of which was unclear as communications out of the White House during the Trump administration have generally implied zero strategy whatsoever.

Nevertheless, Hicks was known within the administration as the 'Trump whisperer' for her ability to calm the president when he was angry—that is, most of the time—and on some occasions even make him see reason. In early 2018, however, she resigned after it became clear that Trump had entirely lost interest in calming down.*

---

* Her success in leaving the Trump White House voluntarily is an example of what another president might have called the audacity of Hope.

Trump was sad to see her go, however, and seemed to be more affected by her departure than by any other of the many resignations thus far. This was partly due to their close personal bond and trust, and partly because she is an ex-model.

HIV and HPV

HIV and **HPV** are two medical conditions indistinguishable except to the most experienced medical experts.

Trump is unable to distinguish them, according to show-off Bill Gates, who claims the president asked him about the difference between the two conditions on more than one occasion.

Nevertheless, both conditions formed part of what Trump considers his 'personal Vietnam': the perils of sexually transmitted diseases. In 1998, the president boasted about his success in avoiding STDs despite his promiscuity since puberty. Trump's promiscuous odyssey should not be confused with the actual Vietnam War, which Trump managed to avoid due to supposed bone spurs (not to be mistaken for the boners that featured in Trump's 'personal Vietnam'). During this conversation on Howard Stern's radio program, Trump described himself as a 'brave soldier', and bragged that he should receive the Congressional Medal of Honor for his sexual exploits, which shows his failure to understand both Congress and honour.

Trump International Hotel, Washington, D.C.

The Old Post Office, located at 1100 Pennsylvania Avenue, is now known as the **Trump International Hotel, Washington, D.C.** It is the second government property under Trump control on that street, after 1600.

History

Congress approved the site for the city's new post office in 1890. The scheme was intended to revitalise the area between Congress and the White House, which was known as Murder Bay because legislation often died in between those two buildings, courtesy of the co-equal design of the United States Constitution.

It soon became clear that the building was inadequate as a post office, at only a fifth of the size the postmaster had requested. It was over-crowded a year after it opened, and the construction was so shoddy that the postmaster died after falling down an inadequately cordoned-off lift shaft, a punishment that Trump would later demand for the head of the US Postal Service because of its 'unfair' deal with Amazon.

Consequently, a mere fourteen years after the building was constructed, the Postal Service decided to return it to sender. Between 1914 and the 1970s, Congress and the White House considered tearing it down in the interests of building an architecturally harmonious Federal Triangle, but, as is standard in Washington, agreement could not be reached. The final attempt to demolish it under Richard Nixon failed in 1972, and Nixon was left to demolish his own presidency instead.

The building has now been placed under heritage protection, meaning that this disastrous, unsuitable building's survival is now guaranteed by federal law.

Eventually, the General Services Administration decided to redevelop the Old Post Office as a hotel, and given it was an obnoxiously grandiose yet impractical building that nevertheless couldn't be demolished, there was only one obvious client to lease it to: the owner of Mar-a-Lago. In 2012, the Trump Organization's bid to take over the building was approved, and DJT Holdings LLC was given a 60-year lease.

Trump redevelopment

The Trump Organization promised to spend $200 million redeveloping the building, and after lengthy negotiations during which heritage authorities said 'No' a lot, the new hotel opened in September 2016.

Among the features it boasts are:

- **The Spa by Ivanka Trump**, which specialises in treatments where you have to close your eyes and hold your nose. It also boasts a Himalayan salt chamber inspired by Jared Kushner's enormous mountain of debt.
- **BLT Prime** is the city's only steakhouse named after a dish that does not involve steak. Unlike most steakhouses, the chef is willing to ruin your $110 wagyu steak by cooking it well done, as the restaurant is owned by Donald Trump, whose fondness for expensive steak has not prevented him from eating it like he did when he was six. Curiously, its list of three-dollar steak sauces does not include what Trump considers the world's most luxurious condiment: ketchup.
- **Benjamin Bar and Lounge** makes explicit the purpose of the entire hotel, which is all about the Benjamins; its cheapest cocktail is $24. The bar is known for champagne sabering, which involves opening

the bottle by removing the top with a large knife, because naturally that's the best way to open extremely expensive pressurised liquid. This service is free, and you'd want it to be since the cheapest bottle is $159. Sabering inevitably spills some of the champagne, which is all part of the display of wealth. The establishment also serves wine in crystal spoons because it's a bar for rich people.

- **Presidential ballroom**—Normally, this adjective is used by hoteliers to try to make something seem posher than it is, rather than because it's literally owned by a president, but in this case both uses apply. The room is column-free, which both makes it ideal for functions and greatly pleases Trump, who despises most columnists.

- **Lincoln Library and Jefferson Study**—These two charming historical touches were introduced as part of the renovation, despite being ironic in a building owned by America's least scholarly president.

- **Trump Kids**—The hotel offers a full program for kids, where every young guest can be treated as luxuriously as one of Donald Trump's very own children, which is to say raised exclusively by their mother until they're old enough to work for him.

- **Trump Attaché**—A program by which 'every request can be granted, no matter how specific'. This would be useful if, for instance, a very special guest wanted to entertain some other special friends and have a waterproof mattress urgently but discreetly installed in the Presidential Suite.

- **Anti-Trump protest site**—Though not billed as an official feature of the hotel, the existence of the Trump International has provided a convenient staging post for rallies against the Trump administration.

Critical reaction

Reactions to the Trump International Hotel, Washington, D.C. have been mixed:

- 'This is a gorgeous room, a total genius must have built this place.'—Donald Trump
- 'An absolutely stunning hotel. I encourage you to go there if you haven't yet.'—Former White House Press Secretary Sean Spicer, promoting a private business while working for the government
- 'It's wildly inappropriate for him to be running a hotel that he's leasing from the federal government. As a president, you shouldn't be doing business with the United States government. He's his own landlord at this point.'—Walter Shaub, former director of the Office of Government Ethics
- 'A frightful dump'—*Vanity Fair*
- 'Third worst hotel in the world'—*Luxury Travel Intelligence*
- 'Shithole'—hundreds of revenge-seeking Yelp reviewers with African heritage

Finances

Trump's financial disclosure report of May 2018 stated that the hotel earned him $40 million in 2017. Although it's impossible to compare this figure with what he would have earned without getting elected, the many customers from foreign governments staying in the most luxurious suites—among them delegations from the Saudi, Malaysian and Kuwaiti governments—have certainly raised ethical questions. The hotel is also used by lobbyists, and some departments of the Federal Government itself, while the Republican Party's use of Trump's properties has increased more than tenfold since the 2014 election cycle.

A failure as a post office, the building has finally found a purpose for which it is suited—enabling lobbyists, businesses and foreign governments to curry favour with the president. *(Mike Peel)*

In 2017, the *Washington Post* reported that the hotel's average room rate was $652, about 50 per cent more than comparable properties. And reviews suggest the hotel isn't also 50 per cent better.

Despite the ethical problems and the artificially inflated income, it cannot be denied that at least one of Trump's Washington projects is a success.

Ivana Trump

Ivana Trump was the first wife of Donald Trump and, an Eastern European model herself, the prototype for Melania Trump. Although she did the world a disservice by bringing Eric and Donald Junior into existence, she also provided us with Trump's best nickname—The Donald—which perfectly captures his preposterous self-importance.

Since their divorce, Ivana has become almost as good as her ex-husband at supplying the media with juicy quotes, and has argued that as the first wife of the president, she is the real first lady. She also claims to have turned down the position of ambassador to the land of her birth, the Czech Republic, which seems both really quite unethical and a cool idea.

She has never plagiarised Michelle Obama.

Ivanka Trump

The president's eldest daughter, **Ivanka Trump**, was born, on 30 October 1981, as Ivana Marie Trump, to his first ex-wife, who is also called Ivana Trump. She has the good fortune to use her nickname Ivanka, instead of being known as Ivana Trump Junior. Besides, unlike her brother Donald Junior, she isn't conspicuously less competent and successful than her namesake.[*]

As the president's favourite and, he would say, hottest daughter, Ivanka has long been involved in the full gamut of his activities, from her boardroom appearances on *The Apprentice* to her involvement in negotiating property

---

[*]   Except in the categories of extramarital affairs and divorces, where Don Junior seems to be a chip off the ole block.

deals with ethically dubious businessmen in impoverished, corrupt countries.

She also occasionally features in Trump's lifelong project of sleazy behaviour towards young women, as one of its most consistent targets. Whether it's the many photographs of her as an adolescent on his lap, his apparent grab of her buttocks at the 2016 Republican National Convention, or his boast that if she wasn't his daughter they'd probably be dating, Donald Trump has frequently taken the role of the 'loving father' entirely too literally.

Though she opposes her father's policy, Ivanka is nevertheless often tempted to separate herself from him. *(Michael Vadon)*

She also shares her father's interest in 'women who work', although in her case it means offering fashion products and lifestyle advice for women in the workplace, as opposed to her father's reported links with working girls.

Career

In 2005, she managed to secure the position of executive vice-president of development and acquisitions at the Trump Organization after an uncompetitive interview process, and even though Donald Junior and Eric already held that same title.

Fashion

She subsequently developed her own line of jewellery, Ivanka Trump Fine Jewelry, so called because market research found that 'Ivanka Trump' alone didn't imply fineness, although her father has disputed this.

Ivanka also has her own fashion label that manufactures clothes, shoes, handbags and accessories overseas, as foreign manufacturing is widely recognised to be the best method of making America great again. Her brand has been accused of copying from other designers, which is embarrassing for Ivanka, and even more embarrassing for those designers.

In 2016, some of her scarves were recalled by the US Consumer Product Safety Commission after the discovery that they were highly flammable. Apparently the premium luxury lifestyle promoted by Ivanka Trump equates to 100 per cent rayon.

Television

In 2007, Ivanka joined season six of *The Apprentice* as a judge and was an instant success with viewers, who were pleasantly surprised to encounter a member of the Trump family talking calmly and in complete sentences.

Political involvement

Campaign

In 2015, her father launched his presidential campaign, and she endorsed him despite being a lifelong Democrat. She continued to support him, appearing at times as his surrogate during the campaign. Donald J. Trump named Ivanka his leading adviser on 'women's health and women', which was to say he didn't have any qualified advisers on women's health and women, almost never talked about those issues and had no meaningful policies in the area. However, Trump's decision to largely ignore women's issues and give his female daughter a token 'womanish' role at least constituted a textbook example of the kinds of problems that awareness of women's issues is designed to address.

Her speech at the 2016 Republican National Convention failed to soften her father's image, but did succeed in marketing the dress she wore, which went on sale at Macy's immediately afterwards.

Trump administration

After her father won the election, there was speculation about whether Ivanka would be involved in the administration, or perhaps even play the role of de facto first lady, especially as Melania initially remained in New York so her son Barron could finish the school year. Ivanka later clarified that she did not want to be considered any kind of first lady substitute, to her father's great disappointment.

Ivanka was officially appointed as adviser to the president two months after the inauguration. Although the precise boundaries of her role are nebulous, she regularly meets with world leaders in her own right, just like a princess would, and it's often reported that her father is slightly less willing to ignore her advice than everybody else's.

Michael Wolff's book *Fire and Fury* claimed that Ivanka and her husband Jared have a deal that she will be the one who runs for president in the future—which makes sense, as she's far more famous, and also the only one of the couple who has ever been heard speaking in public. Given the reaction to her role in the White House, however, she is unlikely to pick up the feminist vote.

Personal life

During college, Ivanka dated investment banker Greg Hersch for four years, and then New York film producer James 'Bingo' Gubelmann, before getting together with somebody more painful even than somebody nick-named 'Bingo'. She married fellow professional inheritor Jared Kushner in 2009. Unlike Donald Trump, however, Jared is extremely quiet, to the point of shyness. Insiders say that this significant contrast between the two men is not a coincidence.

Trump converted to Orthodox Judaism in order to marry Kushner, while her husband converted to taking Donald Trump seriously. Ivanka has three children—Arabella, Joseph and Theodore—as well as Jared, who is yet to go through puberty.

 Donald J. Trump
@realDonaldTrump

I regret saying that if Ivanka wasn't my daughter, I'd probably be dating her. She's too old for me nowadays.

Jerusalem

Jerusalem is the site of a US consulate that President Trump controver-sially converted into an embassy—in consequence of which, thousands of Palestinians were converted from healthy and alive to injured, and at least 52 of them to dead.

This relocation, though mandated by Congress, had been deferred for decades in light of the unstable security situation. But this is precisely the kind of on-the-ground intelligence, informed by long experience of the risks involved in upsetting the region's delicate security balance, that has been superseded in American foreign policy by Donald Trump's gut.

The president wanted to send appropriate emissaries to mark the significance of the occasion, but instead sent Ivanka Trump and Jared Kushner. Ivanka made some cheery remarks betraying no understanding of the geopolitical complexities playing out around her, as per usual, while Jared barely spoke, also as per usual.

Despite the huge fanfare surrounding the embassy relocation, it ultimately emerged that the only thing being relocated was the ambassador himself and fewer than half a dozen support staff, who would be moving to a much smaller pre-existing consular facility in Jerusalem that already provided passport renewals and visa services.

Ivanka applauds as the Trump brand is applied to yet another new building project—note how the president's name is considerably larger than the words 'Jerusalem, Israel'. Not pictured: ensuing deadly violence. *(Josh Rogin/Twitter)*

The rest of the 850 consular staff would remain at the former embassy location in Tel Aviv for at least four years. The major achievement of Trump's relocation thus far, therefore, has been to move the ambassador in one of the United States' most important missions away from most of his key staff.

The US also plans to maintain its existing consulate general that handles relations with the Palestinian territory elsewhere in Jerusalem, meaning that even though Jerusalem technically now has an embassy, it also still has a US consulate.

Nevertheless, the move is the biggest shift in the status quo in Jerusalem that the Trump administration has achieved since Jared Kushner was tasked with bringing peace to the Middle East, although the effort can be more accurately described as leaving the Middle East in pieces.

Now that Kushner's crack diplomatic team has at least technically delivered the embassy relocation that the president's ultraconservative donors like casino magnate Sheldon Adelson demanded, they are now free to turn their hands to other tasks, like trying to clean up the catastrophic reaction to their initiative. Once that has been handled, they can start mediating the decades-old conflict in which they just so conspicuously took a side.

Kim Jong-Un

North Korea's leader, **Kim Jong-Un**, aka Little Rocket Man, is either a joke, an existential threat, or a valued partner in peace. His pathetic missiles don't even work properly, and yet constitute a clear and present danger to the national security of the United States.

Former Secretary of State Rex Tillerson wasted his time trying to negotiate with him, because the Trump administration would never meet with a dictator who oppresses his people, except in Singapore on 12 June 2018. Furthermore, President Donald J. Trump would refuse to attend a summit with a vile known murderer, unless it gave him a shot at the Nobel Peace Prize. North Korea's human rights abuses are appalling and Kim cannot even feed his starving people, but then again, if he does a good deal with the United States and gives up his nuclear arsenal, he can remain in power for many years to come.

Any negotiations are bound to end in failure, except if they're such an extraordinary success that they could only have been achieved by the man who wrote *The Art of the Deal*—or the man whose name appears on the cover alongside the name of the guy who really wrote it.

John Kelly

General John F. Kelly was appointed secretary of homeland security because Trump likes having Cabinet members who served in the US military, having not been tragically prevented from doing so by their bone spurs.

Kelly also appealed to Trump because he was experienced with what Trump incorrectly perceives as the greatest threat to the United States homeland: the southern border. Kelly had previously been the commander of the US armed forces in Central and South America and the Caribbean, in which role he had been unable to use America's might to stop illegal immigrants entering the United States, because of trivialities like 'human rights' and 'human decency'. As a civilian at the Department of Homeland Security, he had a similar experience while trying to impose the Muslim ban.

Chief of staff

Kelly was promoted to chief of staff because Trump liked the tough stance he'd brought to homeland security, and because he was a fan of the idea of replacing flimsy Reince Priebus with a tough-talking four-star general who would form a matched pair with Defense Secretary Mattis.

However, when Kelly began imposing military discipline, closing Trump's perpetually open Oval Office door to those he hadn't cleared and insisting on a chain of command instead of the chaotic spontaneity that is Trump's preferred management 'style', the relationship quickly soured. This has been the pattern whenever anybody in the White House has attempted anything besides total subservience to Trump's constantly changing whims.

On the basis of his extensive security experience, Kelly counselled Trump to reverse policies such as his opposition to citizenship for the children of illegal immigrants known as Dreamers. As a result, Trump began ignoring and then circumventing his most senior staffer, because while the president enjoyed having a four-star general as his chief of staff, he had no intention of listening to him.

Kelly back in the days when he was trusted to implement the mission given to him by his superiors. *(US Government)*

Before long, rumours of Kelly's imminent departure were widespread. In his second year in office, Trump abandoned entirely the practice of listening to his advisors, returning to the unfettered, spontaneous approach that fluked victory in the campaign.

Nevertheless, General Kelly remains in office for now, as Trump is increasingly taking the view that he doesn't need a chief of staff—or, given the number of vacancies that persist in the administration, much in the way of staff at all. This might have encouraged him to keep Kelly in the role, as he at least seems to understand when he's not wanted.

In April 2018, Kelly was reported to have called Trump an idiot, but unlike his former colleague Rex Tillerson, he denied it. This displayed a misplaced loyalty to his commander-in-chief ahead of his own reputation, as there is no danger denying the charge itself.

Like all of Trump's senior staff who aren't related to him, Kelly will ultimately resign or be fired, and go back to being a decorated ex-military hero who made a foolish decision to get involved in politics that significantly tainted his legacy, like Colin Powell before him. Despite his long experience in many of the most significant battlefields around the world, he will always view wrangling Donald Trump as his toughest assignment.

 Donald J. Trump
@realDonaldTrump

General Kelly is a great chief of staff, and a valued member of the White House team, to whom I offer my full conditional support. Just remember what I said about not getting in my way and keeping Ivanka happy, General!

KFC

Donald Trump's Southern strategy for assuaging his presidential hunger, **KFC** has much in common with the president himself: yellowy-orange, oily to the touch and not interested in cutting down on fat. The fast-food chain also appeals to this president because it provides a germophobe-friendly moist towelette.

Connections between Trump and KFC

The connections between Trump and KFC are many. The president is as much of a colonel as Harland Sanders—it's not a military title, but an honorific bestowed by the Commonwealth of Kentucky, in this case for his service to fried chicken. The honour has also been bestowed on Winston Churchill, Ronald Reagan, Jim Beam, Betty White—and Donald Trump, in 2012.

Trump and KFC also both market themselves with a sense of nostalgia. The chicken chain harks back to a simpler time when all a man in a white suit and weird string tie needed to establish a fast-food empire was a deep fryer and eleven secret herbs and spices. And some of Trump's supporters mourn a time when men in white hoods could string up people.

Trump's much-publicised love of KFC works to remind voters that despite his pretensions to luxury and exclusivity, he is still a true man of the people, even though he shocked many during the campaign by eating KFC Original Recipe with a knife and fork aboard his private jet. As every devotee should know, it's standard practice to eat KFC with your fingers, in order to get that distinct oily residue only obtained by dining with the colonel or rebuilding a car engine.

Following the trend established by the fast-food chain during cricket matches, it must also be acknowledged that the president of the United States would also look less ridiculous with a KFC bucket on his head.

 Donald J. Trump
@realDonaldTrump

KFC is finger lickin' good, although as a germophobe I would never lick anybody's fingers, even my own.* I am proud to be a Colonel, like Colonel Sanders, and am proud of the other title I got without serving in the military, Commander-In-Chief.

Kleptocracy

A **kleptocracy** is a government with a corrupt leader—a kleptocrat—who uses political office to illicitly gain personal wealth. Often, as in the case of Ferdinand Marcos in the Philippines or Suharto in Indonesia, this involves directly embezzling public money. However, the term can also describe a system in which rulers enrich themselves by improperly favouring their cronies when they make public decisions. Such a system might operate if, for instance, a ruler operated a luxury hotel near their official residence in the capital city, where high-value clients could effectively pay the ruler large sums of money by booking suites or function rooms.

Another sign of a kleptocracy would be if the ruler maintained a series of expensive private clubs through which members could buy special access to the ruler and visiting officials and foreign dignitaries. Its operation

---

* As with so many other things, this perception may change when Stormy Daniels is released from her non-disclosure agreement.

would be especially kleptocratic if members of these clubs were preferentially considered for prestigious appointments like ambassadorships, for instance.*

But perhaps the most troubling form of kleptocracy in a Western democracy might occur if the ruler or their family had a complex network of overseas business interests and the ruler tended to make abrupt policy decisions that seemingly favoured the foreign interests who had invested in family projects.

But something like this could never happen in the United States because of its rigorous system of checks and balances, designed so wisely by the Founding Fathers.

That is, unless the ruler were president and thereby formally exempt from ethics rules, and unilaterally decided, against the advice of their ethics lawyers, that they did not need to follow universally accepted conventions like entirely divesting their business interests, or at least keeping them in a blind trust.

Though there's no formal rule requiring this kind of divestment from the head of state, as there is in parliamentary democracies, there is strong social pressure for a president to be an exemplary figure of integrity. This norm has always been thought strong enough to ensure that a president acts with integrity and does not try to profit from their high office, at least until they leave and begin hawking books, consultancies and speaking tours.

---

* Of course, the practice of shonkily appointing major donors to ambassadorships is well known on both sides of American politics. What price diplomatic immunity? Just ask!

Jared Kushner

Jared Corey Kushner is Trump's son-in-law, adviser and occasional nemesis. He has been entrusted with solving the opioid crisis, achieving peace in the Middle East and running the Office of American Innovation, among other things. Nobody really knows what he does.

Very few people have heard Kushner speak. It's understood that he can, but chooses not to while grown-ups are around.

Like his wife, the young Kushner went into the family business, achieving what can generously be described as limited success. Jared and Ivanka were generic wealthy New York liberal Democrats who enjoyed mouthing platitudes about equality while trying to make as much money as possible for their family companies. Then Donald Trump ran for president as a Republican, and suddenly Kushner and his wife were among his most avid supporters. Some have even claimed that Kushner was Trump's de facto campaign director—although in Trump's mind, he was his own campaign director, chief of staff, speechwriter, head strategist and designer of awesome baseball caps. Kushner certainly took on the role of digital media strategist, in which he advised the candidate to focus on Hillary Clinton's digital emails, and organised Facebook campaigns that were successful, but not nearly as beneficial as those that just so happened to be coming out of Eastern Europe.

After the election, Kushner had trouble obtaining a permanent White House security clearance, in part due to the security declaration forms he submitted, on which he repeatedly withheld pertinent information. The first son-in-law met with Russian contacts four times during the campaign and transition, and maintains all of these meetings were entirely proper—although it would be fair to assume that his only role in them was to listen.

Some have derisively likened Jared and Ivanka to a prince and princess in her father's court. This is unfair, as there's absolutely no way they'll be inheriting political power.

Early life

Kushner was born in Livingston, New Jersey, to Seryl, a homemaker, and Charles, a criminal. During high school, the young Jared was a member of the debate team, although his performances were somewhat hampered by his habitual silence.

In 1999, the young Kushner enrolled at Harvard University. Although his marks were below Ivy League standards, his father made multimillion-dollar donations and leaned on a few friendly senators to arrange a meeting with the dean of admissions, in an operation very much worthy of Harvard.* Kushner graduated in 2003 with a bachelor's degree in government—making him one of the more qualified officials in the Trump administration.

Kushner went on to attend his father's alma mater, New York University, to study law and business—learning about business strategy and criminality would be an ideal preparation for his role in the family company.

These studies soon proved especially useful when his father was prosecuted for arranging a prostitute to entrap his brother-in-law and then sending a tape of their sexual encounter to his sister.

---

* This is reported in Daniel Golden's 2006 book *The Price Of Admission*, which claims that in his case, the price was $2.5 million.

Charles Kushner was simultaneously convicted for tax evasion and making illegal campaign contributions. His prosecutor was the future New Jersey governor Chris Christie, who seemed ready to become a central figure in the Trump campaign until he was ousted, abruptly and perhaps not coincidentally, at least according to *The New York Times*.

During his father's trial, Jared was not asked to speak as a witness.

Business career

Kushner Companies

Following Charles' conviction, Jared became CEO of Kushner Companies LLC, singular. In 2007, the company purchased 666 Fifth Avenue for $1.8 billion, which was the record for a single property purchase anywhere in the United States, and almost twice as much per square foot as anybody had ever paid for a Manhattan skyscraper.

While the purchase price was high, the building was not: the architecturally unremarkable building is not even among the hundred tallest in Manhattan, and on completion the building's rental income covered an unusually low 65 per cent of its debt.

The transaction was completed just in time for the onset of the global financial crisis, which caused most major tenants in New York to significantly reduce their office floor space.

But apart from these minor complications, the purchase has been a great success.

Kushner Companies has attempted to restructure the building's troubled finances ever since the purchase was completed. Following Trump's election victory, the Kushners began talking to Chinese and Qatari investors about taking a stake in the building, connections that are being investigated by Robert Mueller, especially since the Trump administration just so happened to decide to support the Gulf states' blockade of Qatar only after the deal with Kushner Companies fell through. Recent reports suggest that the deal may be back on, and as astonishing as it may seem, US policy towards Qatar seems to have warmed in recent months as well.

666 Fifth Avenue. It takes some real out-of-the-box thinking to pay record prices for a property this dull. *(Americasroof)*

'Watch this space' seems to be the approach, especially from the special counsel—but given the problems with the building, it's probably best not to buy this space.

The Kushners ultimately hope to demolish the existing tower and replace it with a far taller 427-metre building, also changing the street address to the less Satanic number 660. At this stage, however, no deal has been done, and a crippling 1.4-billion-dollar mortgage over the property becomes due next year, so the current street number still feels apt.

Publishing

In 2006, Kushner bought the *New York Observer*, a legendary publication that had been home to the Candace Bushnell column that inspired

Sex and the City. Kushner immediately reduced it from a broadsheet to a tabloid, alienated many of the paper's staff members, including its long-serving editor, and destroyed much of its cultural cachet. But the new owner did manage to significantly increase the paper's unflattering coverage of Kushner Companies' real estate rivals.

The *Observer* was one of only a handful of publications worldwide to endorse Trump in the Republican primary, along with Breitbart, Infowars, the *National Enquirer*, the KKK's *The Crusader*, and North Korean state media, which later endorsed 'wise' Trump over 'dull' Clinton.

Jared sold the publication to a family trust as part of his divestment of his assets when he moved to Washington. The day after Trump's election, the paper announced it was discontinuing its print edition, moving to an online-only version called just the *Observer*. So under Kushner's tenure, the prominent *New York Observer* newspaper stopped being a newspaper and severed its connection with the Big Apple, but true to its owner's form, it did continue observing.

Political career

Campaign

Kushner took a central role in his father-in-law's campaign from the outset, and appears to have made a competent and useful contribution, perhaps uniquely in his career. As well as digital strategy, he was involved with fundraising and those elements of social media coordination not directly handled by Russia.

He also served as a speechwriter, as apparently he's better with words spoken by others. Jared is credited with spearheading the choice of Mike

Pence as the vice-presidential candidate; apparently he was the least unsuitable person Trump was willing to work with.

Kushner wrote an open letter defending his father-in-law after he retweeted anti-Semitic imagery, arguing that it was far more likely Trump was ignorant of common symbols like the Star of David than that he bore animosity to his daughter's adopted religion. The missive was widely circulated and largely succeeded in alleviating Trump's publicity problem, even though it was first published in the *New York Observer*.

Kushner's claim has been borne out by the Trump presidency, as, clearly, the group within the Middle East towards which Donald Trump has genuine antipathy is not the Jewish population.

White House

Kushner's appointment as senior advisor was challenged under an anti-nepotism law, but apparently it's only enforced for Cabinet and agency positions, not the West Wing, so the nepotism was allowed to stand. Ivanka only joined the administration once this had been cleared up— Jared's reputation is more expendable.

As the person with Jewish heritage to whom the president is closest, Trump chose Jared to negotiate an end to the decades-long Arab–Israeli conflict. Under his alleged leadership, the Trump administration has successfully relocated the US embassy from Tel Aviv to Jerusalem, which has made a significant impact on peace in the region, although an extremely negative one.

Kushner has also been involved in other negotiations with foreign governments, such as his meeting with the Japanese prime minister while Ivanka's company was negotiating a deal with a subsidiary of the

Japanese government, and meetings with Chinese interests that have attracted the interest of watchdog groups.

Jared Kushner with his mouth closed.
(US Government)

When he is not not bringing about peace in the Middle East, Kushner heads up the White House Office of American Innovation. Trump chose him for the role after being impressed by Jared's display of technical nous in restarting Trump's iPhone. In this role, Jared 'helps' staffers who know far more about the logistics of running a vast public service than he does, by suggesting they shift functions online, which they had already been planning to move.

In the White House, Kushner is also in charge of making the public service operate like the private sector. While he has failed to achieve the efficiency standards of a listed company, he and his father-in-law have managed to bring the nepotistic chaos of a private family company to the federal government.

Another of Kushner's impossibly vast and complex areas of policy responsibility is the opioid crisis, which is causing more than 50,000 US deaths annually. The president expects his son-in-law to solve this tragic, pressing problem right after he makes Israel and Palestine friends and modernises a massive, unwieldy bureaucracy.

After these cakewalks, the first son-in-law has been asked to reform the government's highly complex approach to veterans' affairs, serve as a special liaison to the leaders of Mexico and China, and restart the stalled bipartisan criminal justice reform process.

Recently, in addition to all the other policy priorities with which he has been making no progress, Kushner began working with Kim Kardashian West on federal prison reform, a subject of great interest to him since his billionaire father had to endure a US jail. Admittedly, this is one area of reform that suits Kushner, as he and Ivanka are the only members of the administration with any interest in making the justice system less draconian, or in hanging out with Kim Kardashian West.

Finally, it's also believed it was Jared's sound counsel that convinced Trump to dismiss James Comey, which failed to derail the Russia investigation and instead made an enemy of an FBI director with thorough contemporaneous notes about those times the president asked him to obstruct justice.

Declaration problems

As a public service neophyte, Kushner could of course be forgiven the odd irregularity on his onerous official declarations. For instance, he didn't inform US government ethics investigators that:

- he met Russian officials four times during the campaign and transition, and called the Russian ambassador twice
- at one of these meetings he requested a secure 'back channel' be made available within the Russian consulate so that the Trump team could communicate with the Kremlin, a request that apparently even shocked the Russians who were trying to cultivate him
- he met with the officials of a Russian government-owned bank even though it was the subject of US government sanctions at the time
- along with other senior Trump aides, he met with a Russian agent who claimed she could provide compromising information about Hillary Clinton.

He also neglected to provide a full list of his assets, or mention his exposure to one billion dollars in loans. Kushner has now revised those forms more than 40 times. Arguably, these updates have been his major work project during his time in the West Wing. These repeated errors may be why he was unable to receive a permanent top-level clearance until May 2018.

Jared and his wife may be worth as much as $740 million, depending on the accuracy of the disclosure forms he has filed—which is to say that there's no real way of knowing. Like Ivanka, Kushner takes no salary for his work at the White House, and yet still seems overpaid.

Kushner's lawyer has also admitted that his client has extensively used his personal email address for official White House business. Nobody really cared.

Nevertheless, despite Kushner's absurdly extensive responsibilities and distinct lack of success achieving them, he deserves credit for his one substantial achievement during his time at the White House: opposing Steve Bannon, and eventually getting him ousted when John Kelly became chief of staff. For that, the American people owe Kushner a massive debt. But not quite as much as Kushner's company owes.

 Donald J. Trump  🐦
@realDonaldTrump

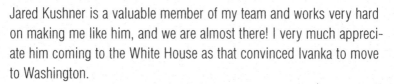
Jared Kushner is a valuable member of my team and works very hard on making me like him, and we are almost there! I very much appreciate him coming to the White House as that convinced Ivanka to move to Washington.

Make America Great Again

Make America Great Again, or #maga as it's abbreviated among the president's legion of rabid Twitter acolytes, was the primary slogan used in Donald Trump's campaign for president. The phrase was devised by Donald Trump himself, and is entirely different from Ronald Reagan's 1980 slogan 'Let's make America great again' and the line Bill Clinton used throughout his 1992 campaign that it was 'time to make America great again'.* Some have suggested that Trump's slogan should been 'Make America Great Again, Again'.

None of these well-known uses by past presidents were sufficient to prevent Trump from trademarking the phrase in 2015.

During the campaign, Trump was rarely seen without a Make America Great Again hat on his head—they served to further his message, to help him connect with his populist audience despite his penchant for expensive albeit ill-fitting suits, and also to prevent sunburn and hair-related embarrassment when boarding aircraft.

It was widely rumoured that Trump's iconic hats were made in China, but this was not in fact the case—they were 'Proudly made in the USA', although in all likelihood by underpaid illegal immigrants who have now been deported. The charge was understandable, however, as the vast majority of Trump's branded items have been made overseas—even his children are products of Germany, the Czech Republic and Slovenia.

---

* Bill Clinton pointed out during the 2016 campaign that Trump's use of the phrase was a coded message to white Southerners that Trump would put them back on top and move others back down—which was ironic given his own use of the term, but nevertheless correct.

Trump plans to use the slogan 'Keep America Great' for his 2020 campaign, as he assumes that he will somehow manage to deliver greatness over the final two years of his term, after his party loses control of Congress.

While Trump may never truly succeed in returning America to greatness, there can be no doubt that he made Americans wear cheap red trucker caps again.

Marla Maples

The second wife of Donald Trump, and prior to that his mistress while he was still married to Ivana, **Marla Maples** was a clear warning sign to Melania about her future husband's approach to fidelity. The affair became public in 1989 after Trump foolhardily attempted to bring his lover on a family holiday to Aspen, and was exposed after Maples subtly said to Ivana, 'I love Donald, do you?'

The relationship produced one child, Tiffany. Trump has confessed to Howard Stern that when Maples told him she was pregnant, he asked her what they were going to do about it, and when she replied that it was the happiest day of their lives, he replied, 'Oh, great'. His relationship with his younger daughter has only marginally improved since.

In her early life, Maples was a beauty pageant contestant, winning Miss Resaca Beach Poster Girl in 1983, and Miss Hawaiian Tropic in 1985. In recent years, she has hosted a radio show featuring astrologers and naturopaths, and recorded an album called *The Endless* featuring special guest stars Deepak Chopra and the Dalai Lama. Her interest in spirituality apparently stemmed from her desire to detox from her materialist years with Donald Trump.

There were rumours that towards the end of their relationship, Maples cheated on Donald Trump with one of his bodyguards—if true, it would make Trump the least-wronged husband in the history of marriage.

Mar-a-Lago

Mar-a-Lago is a resort, National Historic Landmark and ostentatious eyesore in Palm Beach, Florida. After the original owner's attempt to donate it to the American people was rebuffed, Donald Trump bought it on the cheap and turned it into an exclusive club for his fellow painful rich people.

Since he assumed the presidency, Mar-a-Lago has become Trump's favourite venue for weekend trips, during which he leaks state secrets and charges people for access to him.

Inception

Mar-a-Lago, which translates as 'Douchebags by the Sea', was built in the 1920s by cereal heiress Marjorie Merriweather Post, which is why the entire building is cornflake-coloured.

The complex has 126 rooms, 58 bedrooms, 33 bathrooms, twelve fireplaces (despite the year-round Florida sun), and three bomb shelters, which means it could safely be destroyed by aerial bombardment without injuring anyone.

Post had said that all she wanted was a 'little cottage by the sea', which was either ostentatious false modesty or means she was badly duped by her builder. The building's architecture has been described as Hispano-Moresque, which describes a blend of Spanish and North African styles long used for pretentious homes around the Mediterranean, but may also be derived from Post yelling 'More!' whenever she was asked whether the house was big enough.

In an act of generosity and self-importance, Post bequeathed the house to the nation to be used as a winter residence for the president. However, the high cost of maintenance and the good taste of past presidents led to the US government repeatedly declining her offer.

Donald Trump claims he offered Post's heirs $25 million for the property, but was knocked back. So he bought the land between the house and the ocean for $2 million and threatened to build on it, which would have obliterated Mar-a-Lago's view.

The Posts consequently accepted $7 million, yet another illustration of Trump's greatest, and perhaps only, business skill: bullying his way into acquiring property.

When the council knocked back his plan to divide the estate into residential blocks, Trump established the Mar-a-Lago Club. He added a ballroom and tennis courts to the property but otherwise preserved its heritage, because he was required by the concil to preserve its heritage.

Ironically, Trump's purchase of the property and elevation to the presidency has seen Mar-a-Lago become exactly what Marjorie Merriweather Post had always intended—a Winter White House.

Use as president

Even though Mar-a-Lago is around 900 miles from the original White House, Trump has visited frequently as president, from only a fortnight after his inauguration. The following weekend he was back, hosting Japanese Prime Minister Shinzō Abe and conferring about a North Korean missile launch in full view of other diners, because getting a heads-up on global security crises is now one of the benefits of being a Mar-a-Lago member.

Trump was back the following weekend, conducting interviews for a national security adviser, the first of his constant major personnel changes. He spent a fourth consecutive weekend there, took a weekend off, and returned again the next weekend.

Trump entertained Chinese President Xi Jinping at Mar-a-Lago in April, and presided over the bombing of a Syrian airfield from a spare room that had been converted into a secure command post.

The president visited Mar-a-Lago at least ten times during his first year in office. For each visit, major roads were closed, a nautical exclusion zone was established and the nearby airport was shut down, but it was totally worth it for a day or two of schmoozing with his members.

Trump had formerly been highly critical of the public money spent on President Obama's holidays, but the important distinction is that his predecessor hadn't been visiting the Official Winter White House.

Mar-a-Lago Club

Mar-a-Lago is available for weddings, and as a Trump property it's especially suitable for second and third nuptials. There is a spa, a beach club, and even croquet, because rich people.

When Trump was elected president in January 2017, the Mar-a-Lago joining fee of $100,000 immediately doubled. Once one has joined, the ongoing annual fee is $14,000, and staying the night costs $2000. But when you have the chance to schmooze with the president of the United States, who regularly drops into functions, and when at least three members have apparently been considered for ambassadorships, it's clear that in some respects membership is priceless.

Mar-a-Lago is always at its best without any members in sight. *(Library of Congress, Prints & Photographs Division, FL-195-5)*

Walter Shaub, the former head of the United States Office of Government Ethics, has labelled the idea of the president operating an expensive club for customers who might like to buy access to him as 'a symbol of corruption'. Others have pointed out that this is no different from how US politics has always operated, and that at least the president is selling access to a space he personally owns, as opposed to the Lincoln Bedroom.

 Donald J. Trump @
@realDonaldTrump

Mar-a-Lago is a beautiful building, everyone says so, and I am always fielding offers to buy it from Middle Eastern sheiks, Russian oil company founders, casino owning billionaires and other people of quality.

Jim Mattis

Secretary of defense, 20 January 2017–_____

James Norman Mattis is a four-star US general whose most important qualification for defense secretary is his nickname 'Mad Dog'. When choosing somebody to run the world's most formidable military, President Trump believed that the most important criterion was a cool nickname that implies they're a loose cannon.

Trump is also a fan of Mattis's other nickname, which was awarded to him during his time as a colonel in Afghanistan: CHAOS. While his sarcastic underlings invented it as an acronym for 'Colonel Has Another Outstanding Solution', Trump appreciates having a defence secretary whose nickname is reminiscent of the evil organisation from *Get Smart*.

Mattis has rejected some of the president's more unconventional requests, such as deploying the military to defend the southern US border in place of the National Guard. Having served in combat, Mattis is more aware than the president of the dangers involved in putting lives in peril, in the sense that he's aware of them at all.

Though there are concerns about a former general running the US military, most analysts and members of Congress agree that it is vastly preferable to have a defence secretary who seems able to stand up to Trump. Though Trump as commander-in-chief is charged with defending the homeland as his chief responsibility, Mattis performs an invaluable role in defending America and its military from Donald Trump.

McDonald's

The best restaurant available outside a Trump property, **McDonald's** serves real American food that can be enjoyed anywhere, from Air Force One to a king-sized waterproof bed.

Despite rarely venturing to buildings that don't bear his name, Donald J. Trump makes an exception for McDonald's. The president is a long-term fan of fast food, both because of the high fat content and because he can turn up unannounced and get a burger that's just been made, which makes McDonald's an ideal dining option for anyone with a paranoia about poisoning, except via the slow calcification of their arteries.

Trump's signature order is the Big Mac—he usually consumes two.* He appreciates that the Big Mac is tall, and packed with calories, but served

---

* It could be pointed out that this equates to about four regular burgers, but that would seem like fat-shaming.

on a bun with a small circumference—the perfect dining option for a gentleman whose appetite is far larger than his dainty hands.

The commander-in-chief also regularly orders the Filet-o-Fish, and is in fact the only known person to regularly consume them. He appreciates the burger because both the meat and sauce are white.

Trump does not generally order fries, because the potato has its origins south of the border, and he views its visa status as uncertain.

The president's deep affinity with the brand also extends to a mutual fondness for gold: golden arches, golden toilets, and certain other golden options for visits to Russian hotel suites.

The other thing they have in common is that the iconic restaurant chain has as its figurehead a clown with implausible hair, oversized garments and thick face paint, just like the United States of America.

Melania Trump

Melania Trump is the first lady of the United States, but Donald Trump's third lady, at least counting the ones he's been married to.

She was born Melanija Knavs in Slovenia, and is the first naturalised US citizen to become first lady. Her husband is more than happy to relax his anti-immigration stance to accommodate gorgeous models.

She is the mother of the youngest child of Donald Trump—Barron, who was initially a useful pretext for her desire to remain in New York until the end of his school year, or even longer if possible.

Early life

Melanija Knavs was born in Novo Mesto in the former Yugoslavia on 26 April 1970, making her 24 years younger than the president, and just seven years older than Donald Trump Junior. Her mother was a factory worker, and the young Melania determined to do the exact opposite with her life. She studied architecture and design at the University of Ljubljana for one year before dropping out to become a full-time model, for which purpose she changed her surname to its German equivalent, Knauss. She would later adopt another German surname in marrying Donald Trump.

At the age of eighteen, Melania signed with a modelling agency in Milan, and moved to Manhattan when she was 26. She reportedly worked as a paid model before obtaining permission to work in the United States, which her husband must know nothing about, otherwise, for consistency, he would be obliged to deport her.

Relationship with Donald Trump

The young model met the future president in 1998 at the Kit Kat Club, Manhattan's premier nightclub named after a chocolate bar. He had attended the party with a woman called Celina Midelfart,* but approached Melania while his date was in the bathroom—illustrating that Melania was very much forewarned about the loyalty of the man she would later marry.

Melania's modelling career progressed—she appeared on the covers of *Vogue*, *Vanity Fair*, *New York Magazine* and *InStyle Weddings*, a magazine whose advice she evidently ignored when choosing an ostentatious

---

* It's a Norwegian name, and anyone who has anything else to say about it is incredibly puerile.

wedding at Mar-a-Lago. That occurred in January 2005, with Hillary and Bill Clinton in attendance, back when Trump was a prospective donor rather than Hillary Clinton's ultimate nemesis.

Participation in the campaign

Melania kept a low profile throughout the primaries, which is understandable given that English is not her first language, she has a young son to raise, and she clearly doesn't enjoy being in the same place as her husband.

However, she gave the traditional spouse's speech at the party convention where her husband accepted the nomination. She spoke enthusiastically about her home life and the kind of leader her husband would be if he were elected the first African-American president, concluding with a moving passage affirming that the Barack Obama we see today was the same man she fell in love with back in Chicago.

After the election

In several interviews, Melania has stated that her main focus as first lady would be cyberbullying and that she was determined to take concrete steps towards ending this cruel abuse, such as hiding her husband's phone. The first couple have disclosed that the secret of their marriage is they do not share a bedroom, which is entirely understandable from her perspective, but possibly untrue from his—he reportedly shares a bedroom with numerous women.

On 7 May 2018, the first lady announced her first major initiative as first lady: 'Be Best', a campaign for youth wellbeing advocating against bullying and drug use. It does not advocate the correct use of grammar—but it does one-up Michelle Obama's 'Be Better' program. Unfortunately, it was discovered that the official booklet outlining the program contained passages almost identical to those in a booklet released during Obama's presidency in 2014. The program content will be revised, and will now also include warnings against plagiarism.

The only glamorous photo ever taken at the Trump White House.
(White House)

During her tenure as first lady, Melania has often been observed withdrawing from physical contact with the president, swatting his hand away on several occasions. Amid all the commentary about this, it should be remembered that practically nobody understands what she's had to go through during her relationship with Trump, at least outside the Eastern-European-model, ex-*Playboy*-model and porn-star communities.

Nevertheless, Melania is philosophical about her life's extraordinary trajectory, and reminds herself to be grateful, because even being married to an emotionally neglectful, narcissistic philanderer is better than being stuck in Soviet Yugoslavia.

Donald J. Trump ✔
@realDonaldTrump

Melania is very lucky to be First Lady, and there are many other Top Models who would love to be in her position, as I keep telling her. She is a constant reminder that we need an immigration scheme based on Merit, ie Hotness.

Miss Universe

Miss Universe is one of the world's oldest and most famous beauty pageants, which is to say that it's completely retrograde and should have been abandoned decades ago.

The term 'Miss Universe' was first used by the International Pageant of Pulchritude in 1926, illustrating how fresh and up-to-date the idea still is. It disappeared during the Second World War, but was revived by a swimwear manufacturer in 1952 to demonstrate their interest in world peace and the advancement of women, and definitely not because they were trying to sell skimpy garments.

Like all beauty pageants, Miss Universe provides the public with the opportunity to ogle women while pretending to support the more socially acceptable objective of providing educational opportunities for contestants—which, in practice, are mostly just how to have a career in modelling. Unlike other pageants, however, Miss Universe and its local spin-off, Miss USA, also offered young women the opportunity to be ogled by the pageant's long-time owner, Donald Trump.

Trump's involvement

Donald Trump bought the pageant in 1996 to provide young women with valuable opportunities in life, such as signing with his modelling agency. The entrepreneur was willing to invest time mentoring these lucky ladies by giving them extensive feedback on their bodies and the shortcomings thereof, and by making regular unscheduled visits to the change room. This was intended to prepare the Miss Universe contestants for dealing with situations in which powerful older men suddenly burst in while they were dressing. It also provided Trump with a supply of gross anecdotes for his regular appearances on *The Howard Stern Show*.

In September 2015, the pageant's broadcaster, NBC, severed its relationship with Donald Trump and Miss Universe after he launched his bid for the presidency with comments about illegal immigrants from Mexico, which were deeply racist. Apparently, it was fine with NBC to degrade women for decades by broadcasting Miss Universe, but Trump degrading the Latino community was totally unacceptable.

Three days later, Trump sold the pageant, but it's understood that as commander-in-chief he still asserts the right to burst into change rooms.

Trump Mortgage

Of all the speculative businesses to have had the Trump brand slapped on them, **Trump Mortgage** seems one of the more sensible directions for a company that primarily developed and marketed residential property, as opposed to vodka or an airline. The Trump Organization potentially acting as both vendor and mortgage broker might have seemed a significant conflict of interest by the standards of the property industry, but by Trump standards it was barely problematic at all.

Trump Mortgage turned out to be just another Trump-branded business that its namesake took complete credit for when it appeared to be successful, and then washed his hands of when it wasn't, claiming it was only a licensing deal and that he hadn't even wanted to be in the mortgage business to begin with, so there.

Origins

Although by 2006, many experts were sounding alarm bells about the potential collapse of the US housing market, Trump rejected these concerns and put his name on a company offering property loans. In April of that year, when the company launched, he told an interviewer on CNN that real estate 'was going to be strong for a very long time to come'.

By September, the company was licensed to operate in 25 states and claimed to be the fastest-growing supplier of commercial and residential mortgages in America. It would also become one of the fastest to go out of business.

Closure

The Trump Mortgage website claimed that its CEO, E.J. Ridings, had fifteen years of industry experience and had worked for a top investment bank—but, as was revealed in an embarrassing exposé in *Money* magazine shortly before the company went under, that turned out to have been for just six months. His time as a stockbroker had been for a mere six days, while some items on his resumé had been entirely invented.

While making things up to show someone in a good light is standard practice at the Trump Organization, it's frowned upon in the finance industry.

The business ultimately performed far below its lofty predictions of $100 billion in mortgages, and closed in August 2007 after only 18 months, courtesy of poor performance and the negative publicity caused by Ridings' exaggerations. Some bills were left unpaid.

Trump claimed that his involvement had been limited to brand licensing and that he'd never wanted to be involved in the mortgage industry to begin with. 'The mortgage business is not a business I particularly liked or wanted to be part of in a very big way,' he told *Crain's New York Business*, which is presumably why he had earlier written in his autobiography *Trump 101*, 'I expect Trump Mortgage to be an effective company, and it makes sense. A lot of things I am doing now are things I thought of but had to postpone until the time was right.'

Trump subsequently told MSNBC that he had warned many people about the imminent subprime mortgage crash because 'I'm pretty good at that stuff'—which is true if 'that stuff' means modifying history to match a fictitious narrative of perpetual success.

The future president must have been ever so upset, then, that the picture of him on the company website with the banner 'Talk to my real estate professionals now!' didn't specify that they were technically in no way *his*, a mistaken impression compounded by his decision to give Trump Mortgage a floor in one of his most iconic buildings. Anybody might have leaped to the false conclusion that Trump Mortgage, located in the Trump Building at 40 Wall Street, was a business signficantly involving Donald Trump.

Aftermath

On the day that Trump Mortgage closed, Trump inked a deal with First Meridian Mortgage that allowed it to market its business as Trump Financial. However, it too closed after a couple of years and First Meridian reverted to its original name.

Ultimately, Trump Mortgage proved to be a highly subprime business. At a difficult time in the real-estate sector, customers didn't want to take out loans with a company named after a guy famous for taking outlandish financial risks.

Robert Mueller

Robert Swan Mueller was the sixth director of the Federal Bureau of Investigation, serving Presidents Bush and Obama from 2001 till 2013. He was appointed special counsel in May 2017 by Deputy Attorney General Rod Rosenstein to investigate links between the Russian government and the Trump campaign. Mueller will ultimately be fired by President Donald J. Trump for investigating links between the Russian government and the Trump campaign.

Narcissistic personality disorder

A **narcissistic personality disorder** is a psychiatric condition that generally involves a long-term lack of empathy coupled with extreme self-importance and an excessive need for admiration. It is also known as megalomania, or in one well-known case, #magalomania.

Symptoms

According to the American Psychiatric Association's *Diagnostic and Statistical Manual*, people with narcissistic personality disorder tend to display one or more of the following behaviours:

- **grandiosity**, which might be expressed, to choose a random example, by building an enormous golden skyscraper with one's name on it
- **fantasies of power, success, intelligence and attractiveness**, as in, for instance, someone who would run for president without any political experience whatsoever, or challenge colleagues to IQ tests, or

constantly describe himself as 'very smart', or repeatedly tell Howard Stern about all the models he's dated

- **self-perception as unique, superior and associated with the very best**, to the point where one might even insist on their toilet being gold, because what better place for a reminder of your extraordinary wealth than the bathroom

- **needing continual admiration from others**, from *Time* magazine, the *Forbes* rich list, the Emmy Awards, *Saturday Night Live*, and so on

- **a sense of entitlement to special treatment and obedience**, such as, by way of illustration, demanding that an FBI director promise personal loyalty, even though it is the precise opposite of what they're supposed to do as head of an independent investigative agency

- **exploitation of others to achieve personal gain**, which might, if one is spitballing, be achieved by luring members of the public to spend $35,000 enrolling at a university named after oneself that is not a genuine university in any way,

- **unwillingness to empathise with the feelings, wishes and needs of others**, for instance, Mexicans, Muslims, Rosie O'Donnell, women in general,

- **intense envy of others**—such as, to cite a few common examples, Barack Obama, Jeff Bezos and Jared Kushner—and the belief that others are envious of them, which could be potentially demonstrated by assembling a coterie of sycophants on national television to vie for the right to work for the business you claim is amazing

- **a pompous and arrogant demeanour**, potentially exhibited by firing almost everyone who works for you, or perhaps by flicking imaginary dandruff off the lapel of the much younger president of France in an obvious dominance ritual.

If a person had just one of these traits, they might be diagnosed with a narcissistic personality disorder—if they had all of them, it would surely be indisputable.

But of course the American Psychiatric Association's Goldwater Rule provides that one should never diagnose a psychological condition without an in-person examination, so these examples are presented purely as hypotheticals.

Treatment of narcissistic personality disorder is considered difficult—but in certain cases impeachment can be an effective remedy.

The Trump Network

The Trump Network combined the integrity of a multilevel marketing scheme with the reputation and business judgement of Donald J. Trump. Among the 'health' products that its agents were encouraged to market to their friends and family were vitamins with questionable benefits, a cancer treatment that did not work, and a Trump-branded urine test.

Yes. There was once such a thing as an official Donald Trump urine test.

History

In 1997, a multilevel marketing company called Ideal Health was founded in Massachusetts. The three founders had worked for another company that operated on this basis, and seeing how profitable it was, decided to form one of their own.

The company sold vitamin supplements that were supposedly tailored to each individual customer's needs, on the basis of a urine test that supposedly diagnosed the customer's condition. Ideal Health recruited an initial round of salespeople who could then make money via direct sales, or by recruiting new salespeople themselves.

By 2004, multiple complaints had been filed with the Federal Trade Commission by disgruntled salespeople who claimed that they had bought products they could not on-sell, which implies that they got ripped off because they were deprived of the opportunity to rip somebody else off.

There was also a Federal Trade Commission lawsuit over a product called Supreme Greens, which falsely claimed to be able to cure cancer, heart disease, arthritis and diabetes, as well as induce weight loss. When the case was settled, one of the defendants was given the option of paying a $65,000 fine, or surrendering his Cadillac Escalade.

Rebranding

In March 2009, Ideal Health concluded a deal to rebrand the company as the Trump Network on the basis that people seeking to improve their physical condition could find no better role model than the presenter of The Apprentice. Trump declined to take a stake in the company, but appeared at its launch event. In his remarks, Trump billed the operation as a chance for those who had suffered as a result of the global financial crisis to rebuild their lives, and earn some extra income. The founders had an even more ambitious goal – to supplant Amway.

The company's range remained much the same, but was repackaged to bear the Trump family crest. The new Trump Network's cheapest marketing kit cost $48, while the $497 package contained enticing instructional CDs and coupons.

The company's key point of difference remained its urine test, known as PrivaTest, which cost $140, and was supposed to be retaken every six months thereafter. The test was mailed to a lab, which would then contact the customer and recommend a personalised course of vitamins. The only flaw in the model was the minor detail that one-off urine tests cannot meaningfully detect vitamin deficiencies.

Trump's involvement quadrupled the number of salespeople signing up to the network, as Trump represents the pinnacle of personal achievement to the kind of person who signs up to a multilevel marketing scheme.

Failure

The uptick in salespeople wasn't enough to guarantee the financial viability of the company, however. In 2011, the deal with Trump lapsed, and in the end the company's three owners filed for bankruptcy.

Trump claimed he was not involved beyond licensing his name and giving occasional motivational speeches, but his company registered various domain names to avoid them being used for critical sites, and the names chosen suggest that somebody had a reasonably good idea of what criticisms would be levelled at him and the Trump Network: TrumpNetworkFraud.com and DonaldTrumpPonziScheme.com.

The other potential explanation for these sites being registered is that Trump intended to set up his own Ponzi scheme.

Wash-up

The remnants of the company were ultimately sold to an organisation called Bioceutica, while the namesake of the Trump Network went on to run the whole US health system. In this role, Donald Trump's primary focus would be attempting to dismantle Obamacare, a heathcare network that, unlike Trump's, offers legitimate healthcare. It's quite possible that Trump's preferred model for fixing US healthcare is some kind of multilevel medical system.

Furthermore, while it is still unclear what happened in that controversial hotel room in Moscow, it cannot be ruled out that any sex workers who allegedly engaged in acts of urination might simply have been undertaking a standard vitamin diagnosis for the Trump Network.

Trump ultimately failed in his bid to Make America Urinate Again. *(CBS News)*

Non-disclosure agreement

Shortly after the election, Trump demanded that his West Wing staff sign a **non-disclosure agreement**, promising not to leak anything to the media. This demand was immediately leaked to the media. The White House counsel privately believed that these agreements were not enforceable anyway, but decided to pick his battles.

The counsel's view about the contracts' unenforceability but decision to go ahead just to get his boss off his back was also leaked.

Use with porn stars

A non-disclosure agreement was also obtained by Trump's lawyer shortly before the presidential election in order to silence a porn star with whom Trump maintains he didn't have a sexual relationship.

Trump's lawyer, Michael Cohen, initially claimed that he did this on his own initiative, without the candidate's knowledge, paying $130,000 of his own money—simply one lawyer's spontaneous charitable gesture to a porn star his client didn't have an affair with. Lawyers are, of course, known for disbursing money with no hope of being recompensed by clients.

It might have been advisable not to use his Trump Organization email address to make the arrangement, however, given his claims that Trump had nothing to do with the payments.

Lawyers in the state of New York aren't allowed to advance money to their clients, so Cohen is in considerable trouble either way. And the attempts to keep the story from being leaked to the media make the lawyer's client look even worse than he already would have for cheating on his wife with a porn star shortly after she gave birth.

Unfortunately, attempts to preserve the privacy of the parties by using aliases such as 'Penny Petersen' and 'David Dennison' were ultimately unsuccessful, but certainly made the contract more amusing when it too was leaked.

Subsequently, Trump's new lawyer, Rudy Giuliani, admitted in a television interview that Trump had reimbursed Cohen for the payment, leading some of the president's supporters to wonder whether Trump should have signed an NDA with Giuliani.

Alternatives to non-disclosure agreements

Other arrangements can be sometimes adopted in an attempt to squash embarrassing stories, such as the *National Enquirer* paying a *Playboy* model to disclose her affair with Trump and then burying the story because the proprietor is friendly with the candidate.

In every scenario, however, it's worth noting that, firstly, these kinds of facts almost always get out in the end, and that when they do, both parties will look much shonkier because they tried to suppress them.

Nuclear football

The **nuclear football** is a briefcase containing the launch codes for the US nuclear arsenal, which travels everywhere with the president so he can launch devastating attacks at a moment's notice. In recent years, however, that function has largely been supplanted by Twitter.

Trump Organization

The **Trump Organization** is the central holding company for the approx-imately five hundred business ventures of Donald J. Trump, including his real-estate empire, licensing arm and, most recently, the US government. The entity's official title is the only aspect of Trump's activities in the private or public sector that involves any kind of organisation.

History

The company was founded in 1923 by Trump's grandmother and father as Elizabeth Trump & Son, which is the one time in recorded history that a Trump male has put a woman before himself.

The business was renamed after it passed into Donald Trump's hands in 1971, and then, upon assuming the presidency in 2017, Trump appointed his two sons, Donald Trump Junior and the other one, to run the company as trustees, which in no way implies that he trusts them.

Trump has promised that in order to limit the capacity for foreign influence over his government, the company would not enter into any new overseas projects besides the multiple ventures already commenced with shonky business partners in Indonesia, Brazil, India, Georgia, Kazakhstan, the Philippines and with the Kushner family.

Some ethics experts accepted Trump's approach once he pointed out that the Trump Organization's dubious foreign business ties are insignificant compared with his administration's connection with Russia.

Major interests

These are just part of the Trump Organization's extensive portfolio, and conflicts, of interests:

- **Trump Towers**—an extensive collection of buildings, primarily in Manhattan, where Trump owns Trump Tower, Trump World Tower, Trump International Hotel and Tower, Trump Park Avenue, and the Trump Building, a name that doesn't exactly distinguish it from all the other Trump buildings. He also owns smaller stakes in several other buildings, which are worth substantially more because they aren't called Trump.

- **Trump Hotels**—including the Trump Hotel in Las Vegas, where the recent scandals involving Steve Wynn now make Trump the least dubious businessman to own an eponymous skyscraper in the city, which is not to say he is not dubious. Trump also leases the Trump International Hotel in Washington, D.C. from the federal government he now runs (*see also* **Trump International Hotel, Washington, D.C.**), which has proven to be both an exciting new property for Trump Hotels and an exciting new case study for ethics lawyers.

- **Scion Hotels**—this business, launched in late 2016, markets lower-priced hotels intended for younger customers. However, since 'scion' means 'a younger member of a wealthy family', many commentators have predicted that this business will fail in the marketplace, as it will remind potential customers of Donald Junior and Eric.

- **Trump Winery**—like many Trump properties, his* vineyards were distressed when he bought them. A wine critic invited by *Vanity Fair* to try the 2015 Trump Meritage also became distressed upon tasting

---

* Trump Winery's website says it's no longer affiliated with Donald Trump or any of his Trump affiliates, and instead is owned by Eric Trump, which makes perfect sense except that he is now running the Trump Organization

it, calling it 'grape jelly with alcohol' and saying it had a 'terrible, fumy, alcoholic nose'. Apparently, the waiter at the Trump Hotel in Washington, D.C. tried hard to turn his guests away from the Trump wines on the menu. The winery's office is based in Charlottesville, Virginia and Trump has claimed that there are good vintages on both sides of the operation, reds and especially whites.

- **Licensing**—many hoteliers have arrangements with Trump to license his name, and the Trump Organization is involved in the design of each hotel to make sure its chintzy gold detailing doesn't fall below the level of tackiness expected of a Trump-branded property. Several partners around the world dropped his name from their hotels after Trump entered politics, however. The owners of the Trump Soho in New York City had paid a significant amount to Trump for the use of his name, but after his election, the dramatic drop-off in business led them to rename their property The Dominick; far classier, anyway.*

- **Investment**—Trump owns an extensive share portfolio, thought to be worth tens of millions, in other businesses like Boeing, Bank of America and Facebook. The value of these investments is closely linked to the fate of the economy he now runs, but even so, this is probably the least problematic of his extensive conflicts of interest.

- **Modelling**—Trump Model Management operated from 1999 to 2017, and reportedly requested US visas for nearly 250 overseas models. After allegations that the company had also employed models without valid visas, the agency was closed down. Trump Models was responsible for signing Paris Hilton as a teenager, which led to Trump's most heinous contribution to reality television before Trump himself began making it.

---

* Mr Dominic Knight is yet to receive any royalties from the use of his valuable brand.

Minor interests

- **GoTrump**—an online travel agency for anybody wishing to Trumpify their holidays. As its offerings were based on Trump's own travel patterns of only visiting Mar-A-Lago and his own golf courses, this business failed.

- **SUCCESS by Donald Trump**—a fragrance launched in 2012, following on from 'Donald Trump the Fragrance' in 2004, which was presumably less of a SUCCESS. Some parfumiers have speculated that the problem with 'Donald Trump the Fragrance' as a brand was that it made it sound as though the purchaser would take on the pungent aroma of an *au naturel* Donald Trump. Trump followed 'SUCCESS' with 'Empire', leveraging his growing interest in white supremacy.

- **Trump Home** once sold primarily gold-coloured home furnishings, and also a perfume diffuser, although, as above, 'Trump' and 'fragrance' are not a profitable association. At one point, Trump-branded mattresses were available—one can only assume they were waterproof.

- **Trump: The Game** was like Monopoly, except that all the banknotes were in denominations of millions and had his face on them. There were other differences: the Trump game was more complicated, less fun and much less commercially successful. Trump: The Game was re-released after the success of *The Apprentice*, but the addition of the phrase 'You're Fired' on the box failed to propel it to commercial success for a second time.

- **Trump Steak**—billed as the world's greatest steak, it was sold through The Sharper Image, a retailer known for selling the kinds of 'high-tech' products that feature in infomercials. It failed to take off, perhaps partly because a few years after its launch, the Trump Steakhouse in Las Vegas was shut down for 51 violations of the health code, including selling duck that was five months old. Or the problem might simply have been that the kind of person who visited The Sharper Image to buy an executive mini golf set with automatic ball return as their boss's Christmas present didn't also want to buy expensive steak.

- **Ivanka Trump**'s various businesses are also housed within the Trump Organization, including Ivanka Trump Fine Jewelry and the Ivanka Trump Lifestyle Collection. These businesses were very profitable until she abandoned them to focus on a considerably less fine venture—her career at the White House.

Controversies[*]

Race

In 1973, the Civil Rights Division of the Department of Justice filed a suit against the Trump Organization claiming that it refused to rent apartments to African-Americans. The company was eventually forced to change its business practices, but the reputation for racial prejudice continued to haunt Trump until 2017, when he proved his commitment to diversity by appointing both of the African-Americans he knows to the federal government. Ben Carson, a brilliant surgeon and not-at-all-brilliant presidential candidate, was tapped as secretary for housing and urban development, in which position he became primarily known for ordering expensive office furniture, while Omarosa Manigault-Newman from *The Apprentice*, a brilliant reality television villainess and less-than-brilliant everything else, also worked at the White House until Trump fired her yet again.[†]

---

[*] The Trump Organization has also been involved in a few financial controversies, which would be embarrassing for most companies, but, by the scale of Trump controversies, are barely worth even acknowledging in a footnote.

[†] Or she resigned—like most things that require credible information from the Trump White House, we'll never know.

Wages

Many contractors and workers have accused the Trump Organization of not paying its bills, or offering a reduced rate by way of settlement. The Trump Organization's response has typically been that it was not required to pay its bills because much of the work looked tacky and had substandard finishes, which might have been convincing were this not the Trump Organization's signature design brief.

Special counsel

Robert Mueller's investigation subpoenaed documents from the Trump Organization, and while it is not yet clear what they were or what they contained, it seems likely that at least some of them must pertain to Donald Trump Junior's extensive contact with potential enemies of the state, such as Russian agents and Wikileaks—since it would have been more appropriate to refer them to the FBI than sit down for a cosy chat.

Pardon power

In the United States, the Constitution grants the **pardon power** exclusively to the president, who may grant pardons or commutations in all federal cases except in impeachment, a restriction that may prove relevant in the near future.

The power recognises that in some cases, due process still does not result in a just outcome, and the president may intervene on behalf of the American people to ensure justice is done.

To assist with this process, and ensure the president's discretion is applied carefully and appropriately, the White House's Office of the Pardon Attorney painstakingly reviews potential cases and issues advice to the president, who generally also consults the attorney general and other senior legal figures.

Use for political cronies

Another use of the pardon power is to exonerate partisan cronies of the president, such as the following pardons issued recently:

Sheriff Joe Arpaio, who refused to follow a court order to stop racially profiling Latinos, and was convicted of contempt of court, but pardoned by Trump before he was even sentenced. Normally pardons take place at least five years after sentencing, to allow due consideration.

Dinesh D'Souza, who was convicted of making an illegal campaign donation in 2012 and a false statement to the FEC, but was nevertheless given a full pardon. D'Souza made a film critical of Hillary Clinton before the 2016 election.

Lewis 'Scooter' Libby, the former chief of staff to Vice President Dick Cheney, was convicted of perjury, lying to the FBI and obstructing justice. Controversially, his sentence had already been commuted by George W. Bush but Trump expunged it entirely. It may be no coincidence that the person who initially chose Libby's special prosecutor was James Comey.

Use for television guests

The presidential pardon may also be exercised for people who have appeared on a president's own television show. The reality-television star-turned-president has stated that he was considering a pardon for the likes of:

Rod Blagojevich, the former governor of Illinois who attempted to sell Barack Obama's vacant Senate seat, and was also a contestant on season nine of *The Celebrity Apprentice*.

Martha Stewart, the home living guru who was convicted of obstructing justice, making false statements and conspiring to lie to insider trading investigators—and hosted *The Apprentice: Martha Stewart*.

Other uses

The pardon power may hypothetically also be used for a president's campaign officials who have been charged by the special counsel, especially if the president is seeking to avoid them flipping and giving evidence against him to avoid prosecution. It could also be used for a president's own family members who might have had problematic meetings with Russian agents promising dirt on political opponents.

Although jurists disagree on this, the pardon power might also be used by a president to pardon himself, which would mean that he was entirely above the law. A president pondering such a drastic move

Evidently, Trump also had considerable contempt for the court. *(US Government)*

may also like to point out on Twitter that he certainly believes he has the right to pardon himself, but maintain that of course he won't need to do so, because he's innocent. No Collusion, Witch Hunt, Fake News.

Mike Pence

Vice president of the United States of America, 20 January 2017–present

Future president of the United States (post impeachment)

Michael Richard Pence is the current vice president of the United States, as opposed to Donald J. Trump, the vices president. Pence is first in line to succeed President Trump if his diet of Russian collusion and cheeseburgers leads to his departure* through impeachment or heart attack.

The vice president is a far-right evangelical Christian who describes himself as a 'principled conservative'. Having signed on to a ticket headed by one of the most conspicuously selfish servants of Mammon in the continental United States, he is also a massive hypocrite.

Pence is a former governor of Indiana, congressman, television and radio host, and the answer to future trivia questions about the name of the ineffectual running mate of the most disastrous president in modern American history.

---

* Stephen Rodrick's excellent 2017 profile of Pence in *Rolling Stone* notes that 19 per cent of vice presidents have ascended to the top job via death or resignation. In Trump's case, it's hard to know which is more likely.

Early life

Mike Pence hails from a family of Irish Catholic Democrats, although he is now none of those things. At college, he studied history and law, the perfect preparation for becoming the sidekick of a president who is likely to make the former by breaking the latter. Pence attended Hanover College at the same time as actor Woody Harrelson, who reportedly had enough fun for both of them.

Although Pence's initial interest in politics was inspired by John F. Kennedy and Martin Luther King, he would soon be born again as the kind of person they both devoted their lives to fighting against. In converting to evangelical Christianity, Pence also converted to far-right Republicanism and, rather presumptuously, ran for Congress almost immediately after leaving law school.

As an up-and-coming Republican, he met President Ronald Reagan at the White House in 1988, an encounter Pence will remember forever. Reagan, however, immediately forgot, thanks not to his failing memory but to Pence's personality.

Media and congressional careers

Shortly after his first failed congressional bid in 1988, Pence was hired by WRCR-FM in Rushville, Indiana, to present a weekly half-hour program, *Washington Update with Mike Pence*. The show consisted of Pence filling his listeners in on all the latest gossip from Washington, D.C., while maintaining the standard Republican pretence of despising the place.

In 1990, Pence lost a second congressional race after it was revealed that he had used campaign funds to pay his mortgage, his credit card bill and golf tournament fees, as well as buying groceries and his wife's car payment. Though this was not technically illegal, the ensuing scandal meant he lost a campaign in which he'd been ahead. 'Not technically illegal' would go on to become the standard for ethical behaviour adopted in the Trump-Pence White House.

Reading the writing on the wall, Pence decided to give up his political ambitions to concentrate on his radio career, and managed to get a daily program on WRCR and a Saturday show on Indianapolis radio, which was ultimately syndicated statewide. Pence liked to describe himself as 'Rush Limbaugh on decaf'—an accurate description of a broadcaster who removed the personality from Limbaugh's program, leaving just the noxious views.

Pence finally won a congressional seat in 2000, running as 'a Christian, a conservative, and a Republican, in that order'—in other words, a Republican. Finding the rational wing of the party not to his liking, he instead joined the Tea Party. In 2006, in keeping with an ambition which greatly exceeded reputation and ability, he announced a run for speaker. He lost.

By the time he left Congress twelve years later, Pence had sponsored an impressive 90 bills—perhaps even more remarkably, not a single one of them became law.

Governor of Indiana

Despite these setbacks, Pence inexplicably concluded that he had more to offer public life. He decided, rather astutely, that he would find more success in an arena where he didn't have to deal with people who weren't from Indiana, and ran for governor.

Despite replacing a popular Republican governor and his strong name recognition, he only narrowly won the race—although his victory may actually have been in spite of his name recognition.

As governor, Pence implemented an extraordinarily thorough far-right Republican wish list. Among the highlights of his time in office were supporting a $70-million rail package using federal stimulus money he'd voted against while a congressman—and that's about it.

The lowlights were many, including when he:

- slashed funding for universities, family and social services and corrections
- implemented a $1.1 billion tax cut
- set up one of the country's largest school-voucher programs
- ended the state's energy efficiency efforts
- boosted the coal industry and refused to reduce emissions
- significantly weakened gun laws
- allowed discrimination against LGBTI people on religious grounds
- imposed additional restrictions on abortion and insisted that any terminated foetus be buried or cremated (later ruled unconstitutional by a federal court)
- tried to set up a publicly funded news service to print positive stories about his administration—this was abandoned after a huge backlash against his publicly funded propaganda.

It may have been this last project that endeared him to Donald Trump as a possible vice president, as Trump strongly believes news outlets should be made to print whatever he wants them to.

2016 campaign

Pence endorsed Ted Cruz in the presidential primaries, because they have many unpleasant beliefs in common, but accepted Donald Trump's offer to be his running mate anyway. Trump chose Pence either because of his merit, or because he had tight links to the Koch brothers, who are among the biggest political donors in the country.

During the campaign, Pence said that his model as vice president would be Dick Cheney, meaning that he would be the one person with a clue what he was doing, and anticipated running the country from a series of secret bunkers. He failed to achieve this, as it's clear nobody is running the country.

After meeting Reagan as a young man, Pence vowed to some day serve another president from the entertainment world with only a vague idea about what's going on. *(US Government)*

There were some days of tension between the presidential and vice-presidential candidates after Trump's lewd *Access Hollywood* remarks were reported, and Pence pulled out of a couple of campaign functions. But he soon reconsidered the balance between his conservative principles and rank opportunism, and later claimed that he had never considered pulling out of the campaign, and indeed that being Trump's running mate was the 'greatest honour of my life'. This surprised many commentators who had previously viewed Pence as, if nothing else, at least honourable.

Vice president of the United States

Pence was elected on 8 November 2016, on Trump's comically oversized coat-tails. The Bible used for his swearing in was open to one of the new vice president's favourite verses, 2 Chronicles 7:14. The passage is about how God is willing to forgive his people's sins, such as serving in an administration headed by Donald Trump.

Shortly afterwards, Pence was tasked with running Trump's transition team, as Jared Kushner wanted Chris Christie out and nobody else from the campaign had Pence's experience in forming an executive government, or indeed any experience in governing at all.

As vice president, he famously walked out of an NFL game to criticise African-American players kneeling during the national anthem. He may yet accomplish a second independent action during his four-year term.

2020 campaign

Pence has already formed a political action committee called the Great America Committee, becoming the only vice president to form his own independent PAC while still in office. This has fuelled rumours that Pence will run for the top job in 2020, either because Trump will not seek a second term or because Pence will launch a primary challenge. When this was reported as a possibility by the *New York Times*, Pence called it 'laughable and absurd'—which makes it seem even more likely, given the nature of the Trump presidency.

Personal life

Pence married his wife, Karen, in 1985. They have three children, which is apparently why he calls her Mother, as opposed to any Oedipal tendencies. They also have a rabbit known as Marlon Bundo, which is officially the only endearing thing about Mike Pence. Comedian John Oliver, who wrote a book about the rabbit, has hypothesised that the Pences would have come up with another name for their pet if they'd been aware of Marlon Brando's bisexuality.

Their faces reflect their enthusiasm for the situation in which they find themselves.
(US Government)

While introducing him at a conservative conference in 2016, Mother explained that Mike likes to wind down on a Friday night with a 'supreme thin crust' pizza and a bottle of alcohol-free beer, which endeared him to the audience and made him sound abominably dull to everyone else.

Mike Pence rule

Besides his extreme blandness, the other reason for Pence's apparent fidelity is his rigid adoption of what was once known as the Billy Graham rule, but is now named for the vice president. Under the Mike Pence rule, a man must not dine with a woman unless his wife is present, and he will not consume alcohol in the company of women unless Mother Pence is in attendance.

Clearly, then, either Pence is so tirelessly horny for extramarital action that he can't trust himself with any opportunity for an illicit shag, or the vice president views himself as so devastatingly atttractive that unless he takes preventive measures, women will be drawn to him in droves.

Donald Trump does not follow the Mike Pence rule.

Reince Priebus

Republican National Committee chairman, 14 January 2011–20 January 2017

White House chief of staff, 20 January 2017–31 July 2017

Utter irrelevance, 2017–current

Trump's first chief of staff was **Reinhold 'Reince' Priebus**, the former chair of the Republican National Committee, and a frequent critic of

Trump throughout his campaign for demonising Mexicans and Muslims, attacking a bereaved military family and joking about sexual assault. He is rumoured to have advised Trump to quit the race after the latter. Priebus's response to Trump typified mainstream Republicanism's reaction: he was repeatedly appalled by him, powerless to stop him, and ultimately concluded that principles were less important than victory.

Priebus agreed to run Trump's White House, in an attempt to bring the maverick candidate inside the Republican fold and manage his relationships with the Republican House and Senate so they could work cohesively to achieve the party's long-frustrated agenda. This was about as successful as his attempts to contain Trump during the campaign.

Instead of corralling Trump, Priebus battled Steve Bannon and Jared Kushner, whom the president treated as Priebus's equals. He also battled with Anthony Scaramucci, who wasn't his equal, but was considerably more charismatic and interesting, and won their tiff for a matter of hours until Priebus's replacement, John Kelly, fired him as well.

Priebus had the shortest tenure of any permanent White House chief of staff, a little over six months, and yet, in terms of his lasting contribution, it's as though he hadn't been there for even that short period. Trump rapidly reduced Priebus from an effective head of the Republican Party to the ineffectual head of nothing much at all.

After leaving the White House, Priebus went on to—actually, it doesn't matter.

Vladimir Putin

Vladimir Vladimirovich Putin is a renowned athlete, people's poet, sexual dynamo, universally admired freedom fighter and the current president of Russia, having returned to the job by popular acclaim in 2012. Though in Russia, 'Vladimirovich' usually denotes a man whose father is called Vladimir, in Putin's case he is named after himself.

Putin was also prime minister of Russia on two occasions, having switched positions to circumvent the term limits that try to keep the Russian people from their yearning for permanent government by Putin. Yet despite all this, he is a humble man who only leads because he is too generous to refuse the heartfelt desires of the Russian people.

Everyone knows Putin is brave, strong and manly, and applauds whenever he takes off his shirt to show everybody his fine Slavic muscles, inspiring punier men to greater physical prowess and delivering lucky women an erotic fantasy treat.*

This virtuous maestro has relieved Russia of the inconvenient instability of fully democratic government. While Western democracies lurch from one crisis to the next—admittedly, many of them facilitated by Russian agents—Putin keeps a firm hand on the wheel, and the other hand on the saddle of the wild stallion he is riding, shirtless.

The enlightened new president of the United States, Donald Trump, has expressed a wish to become friendly with his Russian counterpart. This would be a great thing for the world, and would lead to peace and

---

* The treat is not for gay men, who are banned in Russia.

prosperity, but instead Trump has faced investigations of 'collusion' that will reveal nothing besides Russia's kindness.

If others are friendly with Putin, they too will find that things in life go well for them—for instance, they might win an election even though they were behind in just about every poll. It has been known to happen.

Regardless of whether one considers Putin a hero, a saint, a god, or merely the finest human being in history, one truth cannot be denied even by his nefarious critics: Russia is in a far better position under him than it was under the communists or Tsars.

Early life

On 7 October 1952, a fine gift was made to the people of the Russian Federation, with the birth of Vladimir Putin in Leningrad, now known as St Petersburg, and soon to be renamed St Putingrad.

The young Vladimir emerged from his mother Maria's womb with his arms already bulging with muscles, ready to help defend the homeland. His first act was to wrestle a nearby bear, which he strangled into submission but then nursed back to health, symbolising how he would one day restore the pride and strength of Mother Russia. Only then did he stop to suckle at his virtuous mother's teat, a selfless attitude that continues to this very day.

Putin's mother was a factory worker, labouring for the wellbeing of all Russians, as did his father, Vladimir Senior (named after his son), a member of the 'destruction battalion' of the Soviet internal security agency known as the NKVD. This unit of patriots had the valuable, albeit bloody, job of purging all Soviet citizens who were deemed capitalist or otherwise insufficiently loyal to the communist regime. It is no surprise that young

Vladimir followed his father into the important work of spying on fellow citizens and removing any who were a threat to the Motherland.

But first the young Vladimir would work to perfect his already prodigious body, studying judo, and also SAMBO, the Soviet-developed art of hand-to-hand combat that's considered a legitimate sport when not being used by USSR agents to incapacitate dissenters.

Putin attended School No 193 (now Vladimir Putin School), then High School No 281 (now Vladimir Putin High School), and then enrolled in law at St Petersburg State University (soon to be Vladimir Putin University of Vladimir Putin Studies).

At this point he was forced to join the Communist Party in order to enter university. Putin says he never believed in communism, and always believed in a far better system, where instead of rule by the proletariat through a system of communes, there is instead rule by Putin. However, as a cover for his long-term plan to transition Russia to Putinocratic rule, he joined the KGB upon graduating.

Security career

While in the KGB, Putin monitored foreigners and consular officials, and also served as a spy in Germany under cover of being a translator, all the while yearning to overthrow the Soviet system. He was in Berlin when the wall came down and, although this has never been recognised in the West, it was Putin himself who tore down every brick with his bare, strong hands.

Vladimir Putin in his KGB uniform. See in his eyes how he longs for change!
(Kremlin)

Afterwards, he returned to Leningrad and worked to end communism in Russia as well, although his day-to-day role was to monitor dissident university students. After the August Coup, an attempt to overthrow Gorbachev, Putin resigned from the KGB and, flexing his impressive biceps as a signal of resolve, began his solo mission to save Russia.

He began by serving the mayor of Leningrad, his former university professor Anatoly Sobchak, by advising on external relations. In fact, behind the scenes Putin was the real mayor of Leningrad as, recognising the unique genius of the man who had in fact been more teacher than pupil, Sobchak took Putin's advice unquestioningly.

When Sobchak lost his bid for re-election in 1996, Putin also lost his position but gained a valuable lesson: in a democracy, it is possible for an incumbent to lose. The future president of the world's most powerful country vowed to right this wrong: he, Putin, would perfect democracy, so that the will of the people would always result in the right candidate being elected, regardless of the majority's preference.

Move to Moscow

Sensing that his country urgently needed him, Putin relocated to Moscow in 1996. Not wanting to deprive his fellow citizens of a seat on the train, he sprinted to the capital, covering the 700 kilometres in a mere three hours.

Putin's initial role in Moscow was as deputy chief of the Presidential Property Management Department, which proved the ideal first step towards making the presidency his property. Putin was responsible for transferring the USSR's foreign assets to the new Russian Federation, from where they could be passed on to the country's new class of plutocrats in return for political support.

The following year, President Boris Yeltsin chose Putin as one of his deputy chiefs of staff, the first step to anointing him his presidential successor. This is now seen as the main accomplishment of Yeltsin's presidency, more than transitioning Russia out of communism, and his prodigious vodka consumption.

In May 1998, Yeltsin named Putin first deputy chief of presidential staff for regions, which sparked Putin's long interest in a place that wasn't then a region of Russia but should have been: Crimea.

Two months later, recognising Putin's service as a spy, Yeltsin appointed Putin as chief of the Federal Security Service (FSB), the successor organisation to the KGB.

Just over a year after he was entrusted with the nation's most precious secrets, Putin was appointed deputy prime minister, and later that very day, acting prime minister. That very afternoon, Putin announced a run for president, with Yeltsin's blessing on account of his protégé's sheer virtue, and possibly also the dirt he had gathered about his boss while running the FSB.

On 31 December, the ailing Yeltsin unexpectedly resigned, and Putin became acting president at last. He could begin his true destiny as Russia's saviour. Oh, proud day for the Federation, and the world! To this day, 31 December is a joyful date around the globe, with much street partying, as it marks the anniversary of Putin's ascent to power, and for no other reason.

Acting President Putin's first act was to exempt Yeltsin and his family from prosecution for corruption. It's what any underling would do when his superior kindly steps aside for him, and typical of Putin's thoughtful consideration of those who scratch his back, and don't try to resist when he presents them with 'arguments' for doing as he wishes.

The presidential election had been scheduled for June 2000, but Yeltsin's unexpected departure meant it was brought forward by three months, surprising Putin's rivals. In the meantime, the new acting president won great acclaim for his tough stance on Chechnya, which Putin saved from the embarrassment of leaving the Russian Federation.

The acting president won the election with 53 per cent of the vote, far less than he deserved, even though many Russians still hadn't heard of the man who had successfully fought his way to the top in order to serve them.

At this point, 47 per cent of Russians were exercising their democratic right not to support Putin, a mistake most of them would soon regret, especially the ones who were gaoled or poisoned.

First presidential term, 2000–2004

Putin established a 'grand bargain' with the country's powerful oligarchs, who had hastily and controversially amassed vast wealth during the de-communising process, by allowing them to keep most of their vast power and resources if they supported the new government. This was in the interests of both the government and the oligarchs—the response of the Russian people to this deal is unknown, but no doubt they were happy if Putin was happy.

Second presidential term, 2004–2008

Putin was re-elected with 71 per cent of the vote—the still-significant number who voted against him proving that he wasn't some kind of dictator. He won greater support for his handling of several hostage crises mounted by Chechen terrorists, many of whom were regrettably killed rather than undergoing the fair trial Putin had planned for them.

During this period, the Russian government charged the country's richest man, Mikhail Khodorkovsky, with corruption after he made the mistake of donating to liberal, anti-Putin causes. He was arrested and his oil company bankrupted—the state oil company, Rosneft, then generously bought most of its assets.

In 2006, the journalist Anna Politkovskaya, who had repeatedly embarrassed the government and exposed military corruption in Chechnya, was shot dead in the foyer of her apartment building on Putin's birthday, which really ruined his special day.

Second prime ministership, 2008–2012

After two successful terms as president, Putin decided to give somebody else a turn, reflecting his deep belief in Russia's term limits that forbid anybody from being president for more than two terms. However, when Russia's prime minister and Putin's friend and colleague, Dmitry Medvedev, was elected president, he implored Putin to take his job as prime minister, which Putin reluctantly but patriotically did.

Putin was surprised and touched when Medvedev then nominated him as the United Russia party's presidential candidate for 2012, rather than take a second term himself. Putin won with 63 per cent of the vote. While there were accusations of vote-rigging, ex-KGB man Putin would surely have won considerably more of the vote if he had been rigging the election.

Third presidential term, 2012–2018

Putin returned to the presidency in 2012, beginning what had just been lengthened to a six-year term. This change had been made for the convenience of the Russian people, who would now need to take a day out of their busy lives to re-elect Putin at less regular intervals.

There were some protests against Putin's return, including a Pussy Riot performance, which led to hundreds of arrests for disturbing the peace, not only in Russia but the world peace that Putin is tirelessly delivering. The president's opponents were put in their place by a 130,000-strong pro-Putin rally at Russia's largest stadium, a success only partly marred by claims that attendees had been forced into it by their employers, or had been paid, or had been tricked into thinking they were attending a folk festival.

Protestors oppose Putin. In proof of his kindness, some are still alive today.
(Bogomolov.PL)

In 2014, Putin helped Ukraine by taking the troublesome province of Crimea off its hands. In subsequent years, he has helped allies like the Syrian president Bashar al-Assad and Turkey's Recep Erdoğan fight troublesome separatist groups in their own countries, and also helped America not elect Hillary Clinton.

Fourth presidential term, 2018

Putin was re-elected with more than 76 per cent of the vote, his best result yet, due to his increased popularity, rather than to improvements in his team's skill at electoral fraud.

Hobbies

Russia's extremely free press enjoys delighting the people with reports of Putin's manly hobbies. He has been featured performing martial arts, flying military aircraft, riding horses, jumping bare-chested into a freezing river, tranquilising endangered wild animals, and even attempting to lead endangered birds to safety by piloting a motorised hang glider. The modest Putin nevertheless accepts that his constant heroism will be of interest to his grateful subjects.

Personal life

In 1983, Aeroflot hostess Lyudmila Shkrebneva was given the honour of bearing Putin's children. They had two daughters, Mariya and Yekaterina, as their father was man enough for the entire family. Since their divorce in 2014, Putin has been linked with many glamorous women, including Alina Kabaeva, an Olympic gold medalist nearly as fit as her rumoured man. But Putin will never marry again. His true wife is Russia, and she is a jealous bride.

Real News Update

Tired of the 'fake news' that fails to report his accomplishments to his satisfaction, in July 2017 Donald Trump launched **Real News Update**, a weekly video series that's filmed in a studio at Trump Tower and presented with the uniform positivity of state television from an authoritarian regime. It is hosted by Eric Trump's wife, Lara, as part of the Trump family industrial complex.

It's unclear why the Trump campaign needs to bother with producing its own positive coverage of the president's accomplishments when there's the Fox News channel.

Republican primaries, 2016

Between December 2015 and May 2016, the property developer and political neophyte Donald Trump defied commentators' predictions to defeat sixteen other candidates and secure the Republican nomination for president. It was the most contested GOP primary ever, but Trump ultimately won comfortably by using his celebrity, charisma and a series of highly controversial statements to soak up more media coverage than the other candidates put together, combined with withering personal attacks on his competitors.

Even though there were sixteen alternatives to Trump, the number of reasonably minded, moderate Republican candidates with a genuine chance of becoming the nominee remained zero throughout the contest. They are presented below in order of their inexorable defeat.

Candidates who flamed out before the primaries

Rick Perry, former governor of Texas—Although he succeeded George W. Bush as governor of Texas in 2000, he was unable to repeat the trick of an intellectually limited southern governor bluffing his way into the White House after the departure of a popular, successful Democrat. He was later appointed energy secretary in recognition of his lack of support for alternative energy.

Scott Walker, governor of Wisconsin—While he had come to national prominence for union-busting and surviving a recall election, his intended position as a provocative, far-right bomb thrower was quickly usurped once Trump started talking about walls.

Bobby Jindal, former governor of Louisiana—As the nation's first Indian–American governor, Jindal had once seemed a trailblazer, and had been selected to provide the GOP response to President Obama's first address to Congress, demonstrating that the Republican Party did include some leaders of colour. Over subsequent years, however, he successfully erased every interesting point of difference between himself and every other generic Republican leader, leading to an extremely poor showing in nationwide polls.

Lindsey Graham, senator from South Carolina—As an advocate of a more inclusive Republican Party, with a record of bipartisanship and moderate stances on climate change and immigration reform, Graham was not the man for these times, as was clear when he called Donald Trump a 'jackass', in response to which Trump gave out Graham's mobile phone number during an appearance on Fox News. In a rare gesture of principle, Graham refused to endorse Donald Trump.

George Pataki, former New York governor—One of the most experienced politicians in the race, he had nothing to offer voters besides more than a decade running the country's second-largest state. Consequently, he was knocked out before the primaries.

Candidates who crashed and burned during the primaries

Rick Santorum, former senator from Pennsylvania. Santorum was yet another far-right Tea Party favourite who thought 2016 might be their year and completely failed to compete with the significantly more obnoxious Donald Trump. Santorum was widely hated by liberals for his strident anti-gay rhetoric, leading to one of the most remarkable trolling efforts in internet history, which is why the Wikipedia entry for 'Campaign for the neologism "santorum"' still ranks above 'Rick Santorum' in Google.[*]

Jim Gilmore, former governor of Virginia—Also ran.[†]

Carly Fiorina, former CEO of Hewlett-Packard—The only woman in the Republican field to take on the history-making candidacy of Hillary Clinton, Fiorina provoked intense media debate about whether she had

---

[*] Reading this entry is highly recommended for anybody with a distaste for homophobia and/or curiosity about the by-products of certain forms of lovemaking.

[†] Further information about Jim Gilmore is available in the usual places if genuinely desired, but is not recommended, as life is short.

performed most poorly as a presidential candidate, in her previous California Senate candidate campaign or as CEO of Hewlett-Packard.

The answer was settled in favour of the first option when Ted Cruz announced that if he won the nomination, he would make Fiorina his vice-presidential nominee, but suspended his campaign shortly afterwards, handing victory to Trump. With her trademark political nous, Fiorina's eleventh-hour alliance had locked her out of any chance at the VP slot.

Mike Huckabee, former governor of Arkansas—While this preacher turned politician turned Fox News host was known for his high-profile campaign in 2008, in 2016 Huckabee, for some reason, ran a much more obscure campaign throughout which, despite occasionally playing bass, he was unable to play to the base. His daughter later became Trump's least unsuccessful press secretary *(see* **Sarah Huckabee Sanders***)*.

Chris Christie, governor of New Jersey—At one point, Christie seemed the strongest Republican candidate—a tough-talking, moderate prosecutor turned Republican governor from a very liberal state, with a reputation for getting things done. Then came Bridgegate, which left him unable to cross over from New Jersey to mainstream appeal.

Although Christie had hoped to cut through the field of Republican contenders by telling it like it is, he proved unable to get any traction next to the even less inhibited and far more entertaining Trump, and ultimately became the first contender to endorse his rival, appearing alongside him, silent and defeated, in a baffling performance.

Christie may have hoped his early endorsement of Trump would secure him the vice-presidency, or a Cabinet position, but he was in fact cast aside entirely because he had once performed the significant public service of convicting Jared Kushner's father.

Rand Paul, senator from Kentucky—The continuation of a long and pointless tradition, in which a member of the ultra-libertarian Paul family mounts a futile bid for the GOP nomination.

Jeb Bush, former governor of Florida—As a well-regarded, moderate former governor from a southern swing state, Bush would have been a strong contender for the Republican nomination in any other year, but primary voters in 2016 didn't give a fig about experience or moderate, reasonable candidates.

An even greater problem was the widespread reluctance about electing a third member of the Bush family in only five presidencies, especially since his brother 'Dubya' had left office with miserable approval ratings, a fact his mother bluntly but wisely pointed out in public before he ran.

He attempted to minimise his disqualifying surname by campaigning as 'Jeb!', the exclamation mark somehow still failing to muster excitement. This, coupled with a hangdog appearance and apparent physical exhaustion, led to Trump tellingly mocking him as 'low energy'.

The implosion of his campaign might have offered one of the campaign's few moments of genuine pathos—the humbling of an apparently decent and well-qualified candidate—had his very decision to run not constituted appalling hubris in the first place.

Ben Carson, neurosurgeon—A brilliant, widely respected doctor who had run paediatric neurosurgery at one of America's top hospitals for nearly 30 years, and been awarded the Presidential Medal of Freedom, Carson was drafted into the campaign after an inspiring speech at a prayer breakfast. Once he had formally joined the race, he rapidly trashed his stellar reputation with a series of bizarre campaign appearances where he seemed to be almost entirely disengaged, and made several odd claims, most notoriously that the ancient Egyptian pyramids were built by the biblical figure Joseph as grain stores.* His supporters were shocked to learn that his lifelong focus on paediatric neurosurgery had not given him even passable general knowledge.

During the primary debates, he was the only candidate to whom Trump ever showed any respect, perhaps because he was a fellow political neophyte. While for some, Carson's near total lack of policy nous might have ruled out a career in public service, Trump nominated him as secretary of housing and urban development. This was because despite all of his shortcomings, Carson was the only black person Trump knew besides *Apprentice* contestant Omarosa, and the word 'urban' in the department's name led him to believe it exclusively served African-Americans.

Marco Rubio, senator from Florida. Once lauded as the vibrant, articulate, handsome Latino future of the party, Rubio proved to be an extremely poor campaigner, regurgitating memorised answers that didn't fit the question on several occasions during the debates. Trump insisted on calling him Little Marco, which was both patronising and hypocritical coming from someone whose own hands are famously miniscule.

John Kasich, governor of Ohio. Despite only winning the primary in his own state of Ohio, Kasich remained in the race until a few weeks before the Republican National Convention. This was partly due to his deep contempt for Trump; partly because he was one of the only

---

* Leading to serious doubts about Carson's brain stores.

---

contenders to hold any moderate positions whatsoever; partly on account of sheer stubbornness; and, one can only assume, partly due to his boredom with the job of governing Ohio. There is wide speculation that he will mount a primary challenge to Trump in 2020, because that would both irritate the president and again allow Kasich to spend time out of Ohio.

Ted Cruz, senator from Texas. A boilerplate Tea Party Republican who managed to play down his Cuban origins nearly as successfully as Bobby Jindal disavowed his Hindu roots, Cruz was an early favourite for the nomination, and ultimately finished as Trump's runner-up. That he achieved this despite being intensely disliked by moderate Republicans, independents and even his fellow Republican senators,[*] illustrates that a huge bench of seventeen primary contenders is not necessarily a deep one.

Trump nicknamed him 'Lyin' Ted Cruz', perhaps on a whim, or perhaps because he doesn't know how to spell 'lying'. Like most Trump nicknames, it lacked originality, was fairly lame and yet was extremely effective in undermining its target. Trump also implied that Cruz's father may have had a connection to the Kennedy assassination, a brave allegation coming from someone whose own father was arrested at a riot that involved 1000 KKK members.[†]

Internet speculation that Cruz could have been the notorious Zodiac Killer was perhaps the only truly entertaining aspect of the 2016

---

[*] Fellow senator and candidate Lindsey Graham said, 'If you killed Ted Cruz on the floor of the Senate, and the trial was in the Senate, nobody would convict you,' but stopped short of actually doing so.

[†] To be fairer than Trump was, there is no evidence that Fred Trump was a KKK member.

primary season. The fact that Cruz was born after the first Zodiac murder proved no bar whatsoever to the fun that people had with this on social media. Regrettably, Cruz's attempts to play along with the joke instantly killed it dead.

Sarah Huckabee Sanders

White House deputy press secretary, 20 January 2017–26 July 2017

White House press secretary, 26 July 2017–whenever she's had enough of denying embarrassing stories only to have Trump confirm them

Unlike her predecessors in the Trump administration, **Sarah Huckabee Sanders** is an absolute professional who never loses her cool even though her job is trying to interpret and explain the actions of President Donald J. Trump to the media.

Even when Trump's actions, statements or tweets are contradictory, self-defeating, biased, absurd or involve hush money to porn stars that the president's incompetent new lawyer just admitted their boss repaid even though she spent months denying it, Huckabee Sanders will attempt to defuse any attacks. She does this by cajoling, or blustering, or with outright hostility or by stating that she hasn't yet asked the president about something, a useful tactic when there is a question to which she herself really doesn't want to know the answer.

She is the daughter of preacher and two-time Republican presidential candidate Mike Huckabee, which perhaps explains her willingness to spend time assisting a sinner. It also explains her willingness to work for someone who managed to get elected president. She is not related to Bernie Sanders or Colonel Sanders.

Anthony Scaramucci

Anthony Scaramucci, better known, by his own peculiar insistence, as 'The Mooch', was White House director of communications from 21 July 2017 till 31 July 2017. Despite his short tenure, he was remarkably effective, distracting the media from the erratic mistakes President Trump was making at the time by making his own far more disastrous ones.

Before joining the White House, Scaramucci was a financier at Goldman Sachs for seven years, and then founded his own successful investment firm, SkyBridge Capital. He publicly supported President Barack Obama, and Hillary Clinton's subsequent presidential campaign. In 2015, on Fox Business television, he called Trump a 'hack politician' and his rhetoric 'anti-American and very, very divisive'. He also slammed Trump's call for a border wall and his attacks on Islam, and tweeted that he hoped Hillary would win.

However, his moral flexibility and the tiny pool of citizens with even tangentially relevant experience who were willing to work for Trump led to The Mooch being appointed to the president-elect's transition team in November 2016.

White House career

On 19 June 2017, Trump named Scaramucci chief strategy officer of the Export–Import Bank of the United States, a role for which he was eminently qualified. On 21 July, he was appointed White House communications director, a role for which he was eminently unqualified.

His appointment initially seemed a success because it prompted Sean Spicer's resignation. However, one day after assuming the role, he gave the single most memorable interview by any communications director in the history of the White House. While speaking to Ryan Lizza of the *New Yorker*, he:

- demanded that Lizza reveal who had leaked some news to him, revealing a total lack of understanding of how confidential sources work
- threatened to fire arbitrarily the entire White House communications staff, revealing a total understanding of how the White House works
- suggested that Reince Priebus would shortly leave the White House (subsequently confirmed)
- suggested that Priebus had 'cock-blocked' his appointment for six months (unverifiable, but likely, given Scaramucci's performance in said role)
- suggested that Steve Bannon regularly attempted auto-fellatio (as yet unconfirmed)
- repeatedly referred to himself in the third person as The Mooch
- expressed fury about the 'leak' of his financial disclosure form, for which he also blamed Priebus, apparently unaware the form could be freely obtained by anyone
- told Lizza he was about to 'start tweeting some shit to make [Priebus] crazy' (confirmed, both in terms of the crazy reaction and the 'tweeting some shit')

- vowed to 'fucking kill all the leakers'. (Of course, Scaramucci was himself leaking, while on the record with the *New Yorker*, although it was clear that either he didn't realise this or didn't know what 'off the record' meant.)

Scaramucci was right about Priebus's imminent departure, but he failed to predict his own, being dismissed shortly afterwards by Priebus's replacement, John F. Kelly.

Despite and subsequently because of its brevity, The Mooch's time in the White House remains one of the most entertaining chapters of the Trump presidency. He has the distinction of being the West Wing official to make the most references to penises during their time in office, surpassing even Bill Clinton's White House counsel.

Post-White House career

Scaramucci has since appeared several times on talk shows hosted by left-wing comedians like Stephen Colbert and Bill Maher, apparently retaining his delusion that he's smart enough to handle the media. He has also launched a website called the *Scaramucci Post*, which is like the *Huffington Post* in that it has no involvement from Arianna Huffington, but unlike it in that it's a crappy personal blog he hardly ever updates.

Despite his short and disastrous tenure as a formal adviser to Trump, it appears that the president still regularly consults Scaramucci—or at the very least, Scaramucci regularly implies this during media appearances. Baffled, some have suggested Trump asks The Mooch's opinion in order to do the exact opposite. Others believe that the brash New Yorkers may in fact be 'friends', as by Trump's standards of interpersonal relationships, 'You're fired' is basically a term of endearment.

Personal life

On 24 July 2017, his then-estranged wife, Deirdre Ball, gave birth to his son. Scaramucci didn't manage to see his child until 28 July. In the interim, he was formally appointed as White House communications director and made the phone call that led to his termination. It's unclear how many of his eleven days in the role were spent on paternity leave.

Books

Scaramucci has written several books about investing, and it appears he actually wrote them himself.

Goodbye Gordon Gekko: How to find your fortune without losing your soul (2010)—Scaramucci explains the 'greed is good' mantra from the film *Wall Street* need no longer define successful investors. They can adopt Scaramucci's model: still behave like Gecko, but claim it's ethical instead.

The Little Book of Hedge Funds (2012)—Scaramucci helpfully explains how to invest in hedge funds to people who will never have the means to do so.

Hopping over the Rabbit Hole: How entrepreneurs turn failure into success (2016)—given his tenure at the White House, Scaramucci's fans are expecting him to achieve major, world-changing success any moment now.

Shithole

A term that can be used to describe African countries and not be racist if you can get your political and media allies to claim that they didn't hear you say the word '**shithole**' at all. When pressed, they can elaborate that they might have heard you say 'shithouse countries', which, rather than a term of abuse, they will say is a real-estate term meaning that there is no internal plumbing, so one has to walk outside to the outdoor toilet. The only problem with this explanation is that, in terms of convincing people that you weren't being racist, it's shithouse.

Trump Shuttle

Although it sounds like a minibus service, **Trump Shuttle** was in fact an airline operated by Donald Trump from 1989 to 1992. It is yet another example of Trump's acumen across a broad range of industries beyond property that foreshadowed his success as president—which is to say it was a disaster.

Origin

In the aviation terminology of the 1980s, a 'shuttle' was a short flight between nearby cities in the north-eastern United States. Eastern Air Lines ran highly profitable shuttles between New York, Washington and Boston even while the rest of the airline was losing money, so when it hit financial difficulty, management decided to raise money by selling off its shuttle service as a separate entity, Donald Trump paid $365 million for it, more than the cost of starting a new airline, and decided to reposition the economical shuttle as luxurious, supposedly in keeping with the Trump brand. After the deal, the rest of Eastern Air Lines filed for bankruptcy.

Trump Shuttle launched in June 1989, and initially performed strongly as customers embraced the glitz, the airline boasting some of the first self-service check-in kiosks, as well as in-flight telephone calls, steak meals* and, of course, gold-plated lavatories.

Financial problems

The new airline enjoyed a six-month heyday, which is longer than some of Trump's other new businesses. And this time, the initial financial difficulties were due to external factors: the recession that began in November 1989, followed by the sharp increase in jet fuel prices that followed the Iraqi invasion of Kuwait, meant that costs went up while customer expenditure went down.

But these problems were exacerbated by issues with Trump's casino business, which burnt through money faster than the airline burnt through fuel. Trump Shuttle ran short of cash and by September 1990 could not pay its debts. Trump also faced personal bankruptcy around this time. On the insistence of his bankers, Trump Shuttle was sold in December 1991. It's not known who ended up with the gold toilets.

Legacy

Overall, Trump Shuttle performed as well as its flight to Boston in August 1989 where the landing gear failed, but it can nevertheless boast several unique distinctions within Trump's broader business empire.

Firstly, as it sought to raise cash during the Gulf War, Trump Shuttle won a contract to transport troops between domestic bases within the United

---

* No doubt overcooked and served with tomato ketchup, rendering it unpalatable even by the standards of airline food.

States, constituting the only time that Trump has been actively involved in military service.

Secondly and even more uncharacteristically, in June 1990, Trump Shuttle flew Nelson Mandela on his tour around the United States. Despite this PR coup, Trump insisted on showing people a copy of Mandela's birth certificate throughout the ANC leader's travels, to prove that the legendary freedom fighter had been born in Africa.

Sean Spicer

White House Press Secretary, 21 January 2017–21 July 2018

White House Director of Communications, 2 June 2017–21 July 2018 (acting, unconvincingly)

Sean Maximus Spicer was the greatest press secretary in White House history—certainly far better than any of Obama's press secretaries. Period.

Spicer was also communications director for much of this period, because his talent was so extraordinary that he was capable of doing two demanding jobs himself, and could have handled the chief of staff and president jobs into the bargain, as well as vice president, which is hardly demanding at all.

Pre-White House life and career

Spicer was born on 23 September 1971, emerging from behind his mother's bush after a nine-month delay. He astonished doctors by being the biggest baby in recorded history, which remains true to this day. The crowds of people who flocked to see him in hospital could have filled the National Mall in Washington several times over.

Spicer was raised Catholic, which explains why, having rained hellfire on the press briefing room during his tenure, he's now comfortable asking for, and expecting, forgiveness.

During his years at Connecticut College, the student newspaper referred to him as 'Sean Sphincter'. He complained and sought punishments for those involved,* which did not disprove the validity of the nickname.

A rare occasion when Spicer was not concealed behind shrubbery. *(Gage Skidmore)*

Spicer was and is a public affairs officer in the US Naval Reserve. In a recent training exercise, Commander Spicer called in an F/A-18 air strike on an insubordinate press briefing room.

Role in the Trump administration

On 22 December 2016, Spicer was announced as Trump's White House press secretary. Two days later, he was also named communications director, after evidently misinterpreting Jason Miller's sudden resignation as an opportunity rather than a warning.

In his first official day on the job, on 20 January, Spicer berated the press for grossly underestimating the size of the crowds at Trump's inauguration, stating that in fact the new president had attracted the largest audience

---

* Unlike every other aspect of this entry, this story is not exaggerated.

ever, both in person and via the media, a claim that was plausible enough unless you had been to the event, or seen any photos or footage.

But images clearly showing a significantly smaller crowd were no impediment to Spicer's argument: he just claimed the press had doctored the images. He was assisted in this argument by Kellyanne Conway, who explained that Spicer had presented 'alternative facts'—thereby creating the administration's first viral meme.

On 11 April 2017, Spicer condemned Syrian president Bashar al-Assad's chemical attacks by saying that even Hitler 'didn't . . . sink to using chemical weapons'. Spicer's subsequent regretful apology was widely accepted, as inadvertently forgetting about the Holocaust during Passover seemed entirely consistent with Spicer's abilities.

Although his relationship with the press corps was often adversarial, on the evening of 9 May 2017 Spicer revealed he was primarily driven by fear, when he responded to news of FBI director James Comey's sacking by hiding from the press corps behind some bushes in the White House garden. When he eventually emerged, he insisted he would only brief the journalists off camera, without lighting, meaning that he kept the press in the dark literally as well as figuratively.

Departure

On 21 July 2017, Spicer resigned upon learning of the appointment of Anthony Scaramucci as White House communications director. Although some have interpreted this reaction as sour grapes, many others have applauded Spicer for graciously acknowledging that there was no need for him with the advent of an even more inept communications director.

Spicer has published a memoir, *The Briefing*, which he claims will 'set the record straight' about his time in the White House. Consistent with his time at the press-room podium, it is a work of fiction.

Although his stint in the Trump White House was contentious and controversial, Spicer's earlier period working for the Bush Administration involved at least one moment indisputable media mastery: appearing at the annual Easter Egg Roll dressed as a bunny.

Even after leaving the outfit, Spicer remained the White House bunny. *(Sean Spicer Twitter/Instagram)*

Steele Dossier

In the second half of 2016, the experienced British spy Christopher Steele collected a large dossier of information on Donald Trump and his employees' and family's relationships and collusion with Russia. Trump has denounced all of it as 'fake news', which is to say that many of the allegations have subsequently been proven by journalists or US investig-ators—especially Special Counsel Robert Mueller and the Department of Justice, which has charged dozens of conspirators. What at first seemed an outlandish compilation of stories has increasingly come to seem like a compilation of outlandish facts.

The **Steele Dossier** was prepared for Republican and then Democratic Party clients, as part of the usual campaign opposition research. It was leaked to several news organisations, and ultimately published by BuzzFeed in the form of a listicle, 'OMG, 278 links you won't believe between Donald Trump and Russia'. In some respects, leaks are a major theme of the dossier.

Among the allegations subsequently proven, the dossier claimed that:

- Putin wanted to sow disunity in NATO, which surely didn't require an ex-spy to travel to Moscow to confirm.
- Russian agents were behind the hack of the Democratic National Committee's emails and passed them on to Wikileaks—as detailed in the charges laid against twelve Russian agents in July 2018. The proof of the DNC's bias against Bernie Sanders has led to widespread praise of the organisation by mainstream Democrats, who credit it with saving them from a socialist being nominated.
- The Trump campaign grew angry when it realised Russia wanted to interfere with US democracy. This is consistent with both Trump's constant anger, and his determination not to let anything else take credit for 'his' victory, such as the bizarre dysfunction of the electoral college.
- Trump's lawyer Michael Cohen was involved in illicit payments and then a cover-up. The payments are common knowledge, and while not much was successfully covered up, this may just mean that Cohen is incompetent, which is entirely plausible.

- Paul Manafort managed the conspiracy, which would certainly be consistent with him being located, as at the time of writing, in jail. Of course, this has not prevented Donald Trump from constantly tweeting 'No collusion!'

The dossier's claims which are yet to be confirmed include allegations that:

- Intelligence had been exchanged in both directions over eight years, which seems rather unlikely, as the only meaningful information Trump had to offer in 2008 was about who was favourite to win *The Apprentice*.
- Russia hoped that Trump would destabilise liberal western traditions and alliances even if he were not the nominee. This was a bold gamble, as Trump's attention span is famously poor, as is his ability to maintain loyal, long-term relationships.
- The Kremlin provided Trump with intel on his opponents. It's not clear that his campaign subsequently used this material, however, unless the Russians were involved in developing a series of lame nicknames.
- Property in Moscow had been offered to Trump as a 'sweetener', but he had resisted. This beggars belief somewhat, as the Trump Organization is usually rather amenable to sketchy business propositions. (See the rest of *Trumpedia*.)
- As Trump would not compromise himself by taking the property (and thereby giving Putin leverage over him), Russian operatives instead supplied him with 'extensive sexual services' from local sex workers. If true, this would be inconsistent with Karen McDougal's claim that Trump offered to pay her himself.
- On a visit to the Ritz-Carlton in Moscow, Trump had several women relieve themselves on the bed in the presidential suite, which had previously been visited by the Obamas (and would later be visited by Stephen Colbert), and FSB operatives taped the encounter. If this

is true, it raises horrifying questions of what Trump has done to the bed in the East Wing of the White House since his inauguration.

James Comey has said that Trump was especially interested in the 'pee pee tape' allegation and kept asking him about it. The president has denied it, saying that it was not the kind of thing a germaphobe would do, however this claim seems doubtful—as any germaphobe would know, urine was traditionally used as a disinfectant.

Helsinki meeting

In July 2018, Donald Trump and Vladimir Putin met in the Finnish capital shortly after a contentious NATO meeting. Despite the ongoing fears of collusion, Trump himself was only too happy to claim that his meeting with Putin had been more enjoyable and successful than his encounter with America's traditional allies—and it is certainly true that the allies appeared not to enjoy the meeting at all.

During the press conference, and in a few subsequent media interviews on Fox News, several of the allegations in the Steele Dossier were put to Trump and Putin directly. Trump said he didn't see any reason why Russia would have interfered, which he later tried to walk back by saying he meant to say, 'why Russia wouldn't have interfered'. He then walked back his walk-back by claiming that there were lots of other people out there.

Even though he is not used to dealing with a hostile media, or journalists he is unable to imprison or have assassinated, Putin had far more success in plausibly denying everything on camera. However, as the Russian president pointed out in one answer, he is a former intelligence agent. By contrast, while Trump was certainly a former agent of models, he is not known for intelligence.

Supreme Court

The **Supreme Court of the United States** is the final court of appeal in the American judicial system and is the arbiter of the United States constitution. It has nine justices, and new appointments to the court are often described as the most significant decision a president can make.

That is, unless a hostile senate simply refuses to consider a nominee, as occurred in March 2016 when President Obama nominated the moderate Merrick Garland to take the conservative Antonin Scalia's spot after the latter's death in February of that year. Then, even though the former chair of the judiciary committee, Orrin Hatch, had specifically referred to Garland as someone he would be glad to support, the Republican senate simply refused to schedule any hearings.

First nomination

This allowed the new President Trump to nominate the ultra-conservative Neil Gorsuch to Scalia's seat, meaning that a considerable number of the decisions on the court's 2018 slate went the way of the right-wing justices by a margin of 5–4, with significant impacts on Trump's Muslim ban, which was permitted, and labour rights, which were curtailed, to name two of the more controversial decisions.

Despite the widespread outrage at these extreme tactics, which seem to violate the spirit of the Constitution, there is no means of investigating the theft of a seat on the Supreme Court itself.

To revenge themselves, the next Democrat president and Democratic senate will most likely appoint a slew of ultra-liberal 19-year-olds to a job for life.

Second appointment

When Justice Anthony Kennedy announced his retirement in July 2018, Trump nominated Brett Kavanaugh, who is more conservative than the former 'swing vote' Kennedy, to take his place, potentially cementing the court's conservative dominance for years to come. If he's confirmed, this may place many landmark progressive decisions, such as *Roe v. Wade* which legalised abortion in America, in jeopardy.

Trump's willingness to appoint mainstream right-wing justices to the Supreme Court is often cited as the reason why social conservatives have swung behind his presidency—and is perhaps the only instance where Trump consistently sees eye-to-eye with mainstream Republicans. Left to his own devices, it's assumed that Trump would appoint Justice Anthony Scaramucci, or Justice Ivanka Trump, or most likely of all, a fellow reality television star to become Justice Judge Judy.

3 Doors Down

3 Doors Down were the most prominent band to perform at the inauguration of President Donald Trump. Best known for their 2000 hit single 'Kryptonite'—indeed, only known for their 2000 hit single 'Kryptonite'— 3 Doors Down were invited to the inauguration of Donald Trump because they were willing to perform at the inauguration of Donald Trump.

The first inauguration of President Barack Obama featured U2, Bruce Springsteen,* James Taylor, Aretha Franklin, John Legend, Sheryl Crow, Jon Bon Jovi, Mary J. Blige, Stevie Wonder, will.i.am, Usher, Shakira

---

* To be fair to President Trump, his inauguration did feature a Springsteen cover band.

and Beyoncé, among many others—but he was unable to secure the services of 3 Doors Down.*

Tiffany Trump

Tiffany Ariana Trump is the president's only child with his second wife, Marla Maples. Born in 1993, or eleven years BA (Before *Apprentice*), she is Trump's only (known) child not born to a recent migrant from Eastern Europe.

Tiffany was named after Tiffany & Co—not for romantic reasons, but because her father was able to build Trump Tower by purchasing the air rights above the legendary jewellery store on Fifth Avenue. It's well known within the Trump family that whenever Donald expresses his love for Tiffany, he is referring to this lucrative deal rather than his daughter.

She is the only member of the Trump family not to receive Secret Service protection, as Trump is so indifferent to her that there's no threat of kidnapping or extortion.

Despite their distant relationship, Tiffany spoke at the 2016 Republican National Convention. She was offered the spot because there was a shortage of influential women willing to endorse Trump, and she accepted it because of her family's fundamental belief that there's no such thing as bad publicity, even if it's a tape on which you're bragging about how easily you can molest women now that you're a television star.

---

* You may remember this band from their 2000 hit single 'Kryptonite'.

While the president's youngest daughter has long been overlooked in favour of her more high-profile siblings, it has resulted in the good fortune of not having her father publicly speculate about dating her.

Music career

In 2011, she launched a music career with the single 'Like A Bird', which was, regrettably, worse than Nelly Furtado's earlier 'I'm Like A Bird', and about as good as the Trashmen's song about the bird being the word.

Her attempt to dabble in music is generally seen as an embarrassing career misstep, not unlike running for president of the United States and accidentally winning.

 Donald J. Trump
@realDonaldTrump

Tiffany should feel lucky she was named after a really great deal—and as I often tell her, if she was as valuable as that airspace, she'd get to work in the White House like my #1 daughter. Sad!

Rex Tillerson

Secretary of state, 1 February 2017–31 March 2018

The first of what will undoubtedly be many secretaries of state appointed by the Trump administration, **Rex Tillerson** displayed the deft hand for diplomacy, gift for nuance and deep empathy with the world's poor that one would expect from a man whose previous job was running ExxonMobil.

At first, Tillerson didn't want the job, having accurately identified the shortcomings of the man he'd be working for and the resulting difficulty in joining his Cabinet. He'd also realised that to successfully run the country's foreign affairs, it'd be ideal to have some experience with foreign affairs. However, Tillerson ultimately signed on as secretary of state after his wife told him he was 'supposed to do this'. Tillerson and his wife have now agreed that he never has to do a single thing she asks him to do ever again.

Conflicts with Trump

Although not a conventional choice as secretary of state, Tillerson nevertheless tended to advocate a rational, moderate path, based on the United States' interest in fostering a rules-based international order, reflecting the long consensus on foreign affairs and free trade that has existed across Republican and Democratic administrations. Naturally, this has led to constant conflict with President Trump, who delighted in publicly overruling his chief diplomat.

Among the most public spats were:

- Tillerson publicly disagreeing with Trump's plan to pull out of the Iran nuclear deal—an unusual response from an underling, but a correct one
- Tillerson's curdling remark that the president 'speaks for himself' upon Trump's refusal to condemn the perpetrators of the riot in Charlottesville, although he neglected to note that Trump was also speaking for white supremacists
- a Twitter war over North Korea: when Tillerson wanted to open a dialogue, Trump first said he was wasting his time—tweeting 'Save your energy, Rex'—and then subsequently adopted his plan without

consulting him. Shortly afterwards, Trump ensured that Tillerson saved all of the energy that he had been devoting to the State Department.

Sacking and legacy

As Trump's chief of staff, Jim Kelly, rather insensitively revealed, Tillerson was on the toilet when he learned of his sacking via Twitter. This seems fitting, as it's likely that the presidential tweet sacking Tillerson was also sent from a toilet.

Tillerson didn't even mention the president in his farewell press conference, saying only that the development came as a relief, and that he was looking forward to spending more time with his Exxon stock options.

Though he didn't win a single foreign policy argument with Trump, Tillerson did succeed in reducing the size of the State Department: his tenure inspired 60 per cent of staff members to resign while the amount of new applicants halved.

However, Tillerson's greatest achievement as secretary of state was undoubtedly the rumour that he had referred to his boss as a 'moron', and his refusal to deny it (the one time Tillerson was genuinely speaking on behalf of the American people). In response, Trump publicly challenged Tillerson to an IQ test, which did not have the desired effect of disproving the secretary's observation.

Trump Tower

While there are many Trump Towers around the world, there is only one **Trump Tower**, the iconic skyscraper, international headquarters of the

Trump Organization, principal private residence of Donald J. Trump and symbol of both 1980s excess and the phallus.

The building was designed by Der Scutt, and its overbearing, black-glass appearance won praise from contemporary architecture critics, illustrating what a dark period the 1980s was for architecture criticism. Trump Tower's extensive use of pyramid forms prompted many to liken Trump to a pharaoh of sorts, as has his later tendency to bury advisers alive.

Since Trump became the Republican nominee, the entire tower has had Secret Service protection, making it one of the most secure buildings in the United States. The money spent by the federal and city governments on protecting the building is tens of millions of dollars more than its architectural value, which is nil.

Trump Tower is 58 stories high* and 202 metres tall, and was one of New York City's first mixed-use developments, including an atrium and a shopping precinct that is technically public space. The advantage of this for Trump was that he was allowed to add more stories; the disadvantage was that members of the public were allowed in. This proved especially problematic between his election and inauguration, as journalists could monitor everyone visiting the president-elect by simply sitting near the elevators—a degree of transparency that was quickly terminated after Trump's move to Washington.

The atrium originally contained twelve-metre trees, but the building's namesake personally cut them down because he didn't like how they looked, a foretaste of Trump's environmental policies today.

---

* Trump decided that the top floor would be 68, because he incorrectly calculated that the atrium was the height of ten normal floors.

The tower was the headquarters for Trump's 2016 campaign, is now serving as the headquarters for his 2020 campaign, and will house his 2024 and 2028 campaigns once he has abolished term limits. Trump Tower is also tipped as the location of his presidential library, as that would mean rent would have to be paid from the federal government to the Trump Organization in perpetuity. It may well also be the site of his future home detention.

Controversies during construction

Heritage demolition

Trump Tower took the place of the Bonwit Teller building, a well-known Art Deco structure built in 1929. The demolition was controversial, both because of the architectural merit of the building and because it contained historic architectural features such as two bas-relief sculptures and an ornate grille that the Metropolitan Museum of Art had asked the developer to save for its collection.

Trump had promised them to the museum, but then summarily demolished them after it became clear that their removal would delay the project. He then insisted, through his 'spokesperson' John Barron, that the sculptures in fact had no architectural merit—which was news to the experts at the Met. 'Barron' also insisted the removal would have cost $500,000, even though $32,000 had been quoted. Trump was criticised by the mayor of New York for his philistinism, but argued that Trump Tower was a superior work of art in any case.

Along with his golf courses, these trees on the stepped exterior of Trump Tower are the only part of the natural environment that Donald Trump likes. *(Bryan Ledgard)*

Unpaid labour

According to a number of lawsuits, some of the workers who built Trump Tower were undocumented labourers. However, Trump didn't object, probably because they were white men from Eastern Europe. The Polish builders alleged that they were paid four dollars an hour for a twelve-hour shift, when they were paid at all. They didn't have hard hats, and slept onsite, the first of many Eastern Europeans to spend the night there. Allegedly, a Trump Organization lawyer threatened to have the workers deported when they began their legal action. Trump ultimately paid $1.375 million to make the problem go away, establishing that the best way for a subcontractor to get paid by Donald Trump is a court order.

Other controversies

Construction was halted on two occasions by protesters wanting Trump to hire more minorities—they were ignored, proving that Trump has at least one core value that he hasn't abandoned over the years.

It has been alleged that Trump Tower was built from concrete instead of steel like most skyscrapers because of the involvement of organised crime, which was believed to control New York's concrete market at

Tacky, implausibly vertical and made of cement, Trump Tower is believed to be the inspiration for Donald Trump's hairdo. *(Bin Im Garten)*

the time, leading to the highest prices in America for the raw material. However, this has never been proven, and nor can it be demonstrated that anyone involved ended up wearing concrete boots or, a worse fate still, living in Trump Tower.

In 2017, the City of New York ordered the removal of two unauthorised booths that were selling Trump merchandise in the supposedly public atrium—even in this minor respect, the Trump Organization was unwilling to play by local property rules.

Retail levels

The tower has several retail tenants:

Trump Grill is a traditional American steakhouse where diners can experience premium beefsteak the way Trump himself likes it: ruined by overcooking and slathered in tomato sauce. The burrito bowls that Trump famously tweeted about on Cinco de Mayo in 2016 are the only Mexican food the president has ever eaten.

The **Ivanka Trump Store** opened with considerable fanfare after Nordstrom and other top retailers stopped carrying the future first daughter's handbags. The outlet proved to be extremely small, just 20 feet by six feet. It is more accurately the Ivanka Trump Feature Wall.

Trump Bar is the world's best bar named after a lifelong teetotaller, renowned for stocking many different vintages of Diet Coke.

Trump Cafe serves pizzas, hamburgers, salads and the like. Apparently, Mr Trump's favourite order is his mother's meatloaf, the mainstay of the menu, as he is still in so many respects a child.

Trump's Ice Cream Parlor illustrates that, again, he's a child. Flavours include Vanilla Fudge Swirl (unsurprisingly), Dulce De Leche (surprisingly) and Moose Tracks (incomprehensibly).*

Starbucks's presence is apparently at odds with the 'premium' image intended for Trump Tower, but there is a rule that every single building in New York City must contain a Starbucks.

Gucci is the largest retail tenant, with frontage on Fifth Avenue. As it is a renowned global luxury brand, its presence in Trump Tower is an anomaly.

A feature waterfall described by the Trump Organization as a 'breathtaking 60-foot waterfall'.† It symbolises the now well-known association between Donald Trump and cascading liquids.

Notable current and former residents

Donald and Melania Trump—President and first lady of the United States‡

Paul Manafort—Formerly Trump's campaign manager and charged with fraud by special counsel Robert Mueller. It's not known how he compares the accommodation at Trump Tower with his stay in prison.

Johnny Carson—When on the East Coast, the one-time king of late-night television naturally headquartered himself in a farcical building.

Bruce Willis—The actor bought Carson's apartment, bravely moving into a skyscraper despite starring in *Die Hard*.

---

* Further research reveals that, it's fudge ripple with embedded peanut butter cups, which sounds like the kind of thing Trump would eat, or even invent.

† Although on the Trump Café website, it's now become a 40-foot waterfall.

‡ There are no other notable members of the Trump family.

Andrew Lloyd Webber—His musical *Phantom of the Opera*, about a hideous but powerful man who destructively pursues a much younger, beautiful woman, is thought to have been inspired by the building's namesake.

Liberace—The building's second-most flamboyant, vainglorious resident.

Steven Spielberg—The legendary director's lifelong affinity for outstanding storytelling naturally drew him to President Trump.

Chuck Blazer—The former FIFA official rented one apartment for himself and one for his cats. He later pleaded guilty to tax evasion, money laundering, racketeering and wire fraud, but died before being sentenced.

José Maria Marin—Another former FIFA official, Marin served house arrest in his condo.

Helly Nahmad—Ran a gambling ring from his apartment.

Vadim Trincher—Also ran a gambling ring.

Robert Hopkins—Ran yet another gambling ring, but was also accused of murder. It's almost as though Trump Tower was the headquarters of some kind of criminal organisation.

Steven Hoffenberg—This resident was convicted of running one of the world's largest-ever Ponzi schemes, and later founded a pro-Trump PAC, which might well have had some features in common.

Michael Jackson—Another of the many people who once called Trump Tower home and was charged with serious crimes.

Donald J. Trump for President, Inc—Scene of the notorious 9 June 2016 meeting between Trump campaign officials and suspected Russian agents.

'Baby Doc' Duvalier—The other world leader investigated for serious criminal activity who has owned a condo in Trump Tower.

Twitter

Though it began life as a social network, **Twitter** is now the official organ of the president of the United States, allowing him to make announcements, offer commentary, conduct diplomatic relations and, on occasion, terminate the employment of senior staff. While originally designed to allow users to connect and communicate with one another in real time, Donald Trump has turned Twitter into a broadcasting platform for the immediate, unfiltered, one-way dissemination of his every thought.

With a single tweet, Trump can set the news agenda, bully individuals, create diplomatic tension, threaten military action and cause share prices to nosedive. He has not yet explored the possibility of using the platform for a positive purpose.

Twitter's enforced brevity, its point of difference with other platforms, has proven ideal for capturing Trump's thoughts, which are typically furious kneejerks. Neuroscientists have postulated that Trump's thoughts have never been more complex and nuanced than 140 characters, which is what has allowed this unique symbiosis between message, messenger and platform.

So prolific has Trump been on Twitter over the years that whenever the president makes any major decision or statement, an old tweet immediately resurfaces of him angrily criticising the thing he just did.

Trump's critics have demanded Twitter banish the president: the one instance of the president's free speech being threatened rather than the other way around. Were it to do so, however, Trump would undoubtedly nationalise the service.

Twitter is so essential to Trump's political identity that it's assumed his presidential library will merely archive his tweets, which would also reflect his level of interest in literature, scholarship and other people's opinions.

Trump University

Trump ~~University~~ was a university that did not grade students, confer degrees, was unaccredited and was not a university at all. It was also barely 'Trump', with minimal involvement from its namesake beyond marketing, and majority ownership of the company.

Nevertheless, Trump ~~University~~ provided precisely what it sounds like: an education worthy of Donald Trump himself. The main lesson it taught was that starting a ~~university~~ named after a famous businessman is a good way to make large amounts of money from credulous customers.

Another important lesson taught at Trump ~~University~~ is that if one finds oneself enrolled in a bogus ~~university~~, a class action can provide relief, especially if the ~~university~~'s namesake has just been elected president and needs to tie up loose ends.

Origins

When entrepreneur Michael Sexton pitched a real-estate training program to Donald Trump, with the idea of paying him a fee for the use of his name, Sexton himself learned a valuable business lesson when Trump decided he wanted 93 per cent of the company.

Trump ~~University~~ opened in 2005 with grandiose statements from its namesake about his love of imparting knowledge, including a vow to 'turn anyone into a real-estate investor'. Unfortunately, the knowledge that it's not legal to just call any old business a university had not been imparted to the founders.

Most students' ~~university~~ experience started with a session in a temporarily rented space where they were encouraged to sign up for classes ranging from a $1500 three-day course to a $35,000 'gold elite' program, which supposedly provided a year of seminars and personal mentorship. In practice, this experience amounted to being told they could find information on taxation on the IRS website, and that a good method of finding suitable investment properties was to use a search engine.[*]

Complaints

In an infomercial, Trump claimed that he had personally handpicked the instructors, but in a 2012 deposition, he stated that he had never chosen any of them, providing a useful case study for real university law students learning about misrepresentation, false advertising, passing off, and how people sometimes change their stories under penalty of perjury.

The main expertise of the instructors at Trump ~~University~~, according to multiple reports, was in pressuring students to purchase more seminars, even if they had to go into debt to afford them. Students of the ~~university~~ could have successfully used the techniques they experienced first-hand to launch successful careers selling Tupperware, used cars, timeshare properties or courses at their own eponymous fake university.

---

[*]   This is according to an NPR interview with 76-year-old retiree Bob Guillo, who took $35 000 out of his retirement account to sign up. After complaining, he found himself being attacked by Trump during the campaign, which is more personal attention from the founder than other students received.

Lawsuits and ultimate closure

For a period in 2008, Trump ~~University~~ was renamed the Trump Wealth Institute, a fitting name, although more wealth was accumulated by the operators than the attendees.

In response to a 2010 letter from the New York deputy commissioner for higher education, Trump University was renamed the Trump Entrepreneur Initiative. It closed shortly afterwards. In 2013, the State of New York launched a $40 million suit alleging false claims and illegal business practices. Several federal lawsuits were also launched, one of which alleged racketeering.

In response, Trump argued that the university had a 98 per cent approval rating from its students, although some alleged they had been made to fill out positive feedback forms before being allowed to 'graduate', which you don't need a statistics degree from a legitimate university to suspect might have influenced that figure.

Trump also called the federal judge who presided over the Trump University matter, Judge Gonzalo Curiel, a 'hater' and 'Spanish' or 'Mexican', and said he should recuse himself from the case, asserting that anyone who wasn't white, and especially someone who was Latino, would have a pretty major problem with Trump. This supposition was disproved by exit polls from the 2016 election.

Trump settled all the lawsuits arising from Trump ~~University~~ for $25 million after being elected president, but never admitted any wrongdoing. He tweeted that the 'ONLY bad thing about winning the Presidency is that I did not have the time to go through a long but winning trial on Trump U. Too bad!' This tweet makes it clear that irrespective of the nature of Trump's educational institution, it was certainly not a law school.

Whether they made a bad deal or were the victims of a genuine scam, it would be unfair to say that the students of Trump ~~University~~ seminars got nothing—not when they got to pose next to a life-sized photo of Donald Trump.

Trump Vodka

Trump Vodka was a supposedly premium product launched in 2005 under the tagline 'Success distilled'. It promised to 'Demand the same respect and inspire the same awe as . . . Trump himself.' It achieved this, which is why it was discontinued in 2011.

History

In 2005, the Trump Organization did a deal with Drinks Americas to produce Trump 'Super Premium' Vodka. Donald Trump predicted it would outsell the highly regarded Grey Goose, and claimed that a 'Trump and tonic', or T&T, would become the most popular cocktail in the United States.

If this wasn't ambitious enough, in 2007, Drinks America did a deal to export 50,000 cases of Trump Vodka to Russia each year. It did not sell well—most Russians considered it only fit for pouring onto the bed of somebody they disliked, a traditional Muscovite shaming ritual.

Trump Vodka was discontinued in the United States in 2011 due to insufficient sales. Several reasons for this have been suggested. The first is that the licensor's insistence on using gold leaf for the bottles, supposedly to resemble Trump Tower, made them too expensive to produce.

Trump Vodka was the best way to forget you attended Trump University.

The second obvious problem was that Trump never consumed the product, and indeed is a lifelong teetotaller because he holds alcoholism responsible for the death of his brother, Fred Trump Junior. Apparently, selling a potent spirit bearing the same surname as the deceased was less of a concern.

Israeli success

Trump Vodka is, however, still available in Israel, where it was produced by a local supplier who used Donald Trump's image to market the product, apparently without his consent. Trump initially sued over this, but later cut a deal to allow production to continue.

According to the *Times of Israel*, Trump Vodka is the preferred tipple of Orthodox Jews during Passover, as it's the only vodka made from potatoes rather than grain and is therefore kosher. The decision to substitute potatoes was made by the Israeli distributor/pirate, as the original American vodka was made from grain.

One shopkeeper in Tel Aviv interviewed by the *Times* said they only keep it during Passover, as it doesn't sell well throughout the rest of the year. Another saleswoman said even though it was the only kosher option, she didn't recommend it, due to its 'pungent flavour'.

Trump, of course, has an Orthodox daughter and son-in-law, and while their views on the curious popularity of their father's failed vodka in Israel are not known, Jared Kushner could surely be forgiven if being Donald Trump's son-in-law has driven him to hard liquor.

Voter fraud

Accusations of **voter fraud** in the 2016 election are either legitimate claims that there was an outrageous, criminal conspiracy to deny that Donald J. Trump won the popular vote, or proof of the president's fantasist tendencies when facts fail to concur with his personal narrative of constant success in every venture.

Origins

Trump has repeatedly claimed that millions of illegal immigrants voted in the election, and that in California 'millions and millions of people' voted 'many times'. This followed on the heels of his prediction ahead of election day that the poll would be rigged, and that some voters would even be 'dead (and many for a long time)'. Though these campaign remarks were intended to let him claim that he was the real victor in the event of his defeat, the fact that he was the actual victor seems not to have deterred him from complaining about the vast conspiracy that set out to deny him the election.

Of course, if illegal immigrants had wanted to falsify votes for Hillary Clinton in order to deprive Trump of the presidency, they would have been much wiser to do so in swing states like Michigan, where Trump only narrowly won, rather than in California, which always votes Democrat.*

Commission

Despite there being no evidence of widespread voter fraud occurring in 2016 at all, or indeed ever playing a significant role in the recent history of presidential elections, on 11 May 2017, Trump created the Presidential Advisory Commission on Election Integrity. He appointed Vice President Mike Pence as chair, and Kansas Secretary of State Kris Kobach, a long-term obsessive campaigner against imaginary voter fraud, as vice chair, to investigate this apparent, albeit imaginary, outrage.

There was extensive opposition to the commission, especially after it asked states[†] to supply voters' full names, addresses, dates of birth, social security numbers, party affiliations and voting histories since 2006. This would have allowed the commission and its supporters to track down those who had not supported the president in 2016. This was opposed

---

* If any of the millions of illegal-immigrant vote fraudsters are reading this, they might want to consider that approach next time around.

† States conduct federal voting in the United States, in the absence of an independent body like Australia's electoral commission, because that's a much better system that has never been known to achieve outrageously partisan results—except all the times it has, like the Florida standoff in 2000.

by many states on civil liberties grounds, which for Trump further proved the existence of a sinister leftist conspiracy.

Dissolution

After months of work and hundreds of thousands of dollars, Trump dissolved the commission when it was unable to substantiate his claims. He seemingly took this to mean not that the allegations of voter fraud were a paranoid delusion, but as further evidence of just how deep the conspiracy against him went.

A survey by the Brennan Center for Justice at New York University, which assessed 23 million ballots in disputed areas, found a mere 30 cases of non-citizens voting—but having been produced by a university in a liberal city, that result was easily dismissed as yet another fabrication of the 'deep state'.

Despite every indication that his beliefs are both unfounded and a waste of time, Trump still persists with the belief that millions of illegal immigrants voted for Hillary, somehow beating the security checks despite being ineligible and not enrolled. Then again, he also believes that climate change was invented by the Chinese to give them an economic advantage while the West ties itself in knots trying to fix the environment.

After dissolving his commission, he asked the Department of Homeland Security to take over the 'investigation', as though it doesn't have actual security concerns to address. But Trump's continued obsession with his loss of the popular vote in 2016 gives a strong indication of just how apoplectically he would have reacted if he had lost the actual election, and not been granted the ability to create futile commissions into his non-loss.

Curiously, Trump is much less interested in safeguarding the integrity of elections after seventeen intelligence agencies told him that they were undermined by enemy agents because the Russian government wanted him to win.

The Wall

The Wall has been the central fantasy of Donald Trump's political career campaign, combining his instinctive resentment of foreigners with his property developer's love of enormous, expensive, unnecessary construction.

It is a so-far theoretical wall right across the United States–Mexico border that, in Trump's mind if not in reality, would successfully keep out perceived undesirables such as criminals, terrorists and Mexicans.

Concept

The 'big beautiful wall' remains a core ambition for Trump, regardless of whether it would in fact prevent illegal immigration at the southern border, whether there are already walls there, which have failed to curb illegal immigration, whether cameras, drones or infrared sensors would do a better job for less money, whether improving economic conditions in Mexico would be both more effective and equitable than simply unilaterally blocking the border, and whether there is any realistic chance of constructing a multibillion-dollar wall 3200 kilometres long when the government has a huge deficit recently made even huger by tax cuts.

But if building this wall seems impossible—and it does to everyone besides Trump and his rally crowds—it is highly practical compared with the president's demand that Mexico pay for it, when Mexico does not want a wall, cannot afford a wall, and would deeply resent a wall if it were ever constructed.

Trump's plan to force Mexico to pay for his wall will never be needed, given the unlikelihood of its construction, but his theory is that the United States would impose a 20 per cent tariff on Mexican imports, which would require him to not only trash NAFTA, but would result in Mexico imposing a similar tariff on US imports, thus cancelling out the revenue raised by the first tariff. As a newcomer to macroeconomics, Trump is only now realising that if he imposes a tariff on a foreign country, it will reciprocate, as has occurred with China and others.

As he became increasingly frustrated by the resistance to his plan from Congress, local, state and federal authorities, Mexico and anyone with basic common sense, Trump also suggested that the wall could be covered in solar panels to generate revenue. This is the only time the president has ever supported renewable energy. While this may seem inconsistent with his climate-change scepticism, it seems to be a way of delivering Trump's pledge that the wall wouldn't cost US taxpayers anything while also recognising that Mexico will never pay for it. Trump is belatedly realising that his repeated claims about Mexico funding his hypotheti-wall are beginning to look like yet another fanciful promise from a man who never thought he'd be elected and have to figure out how to deliver it.

The president vowed in August 2017 to close down the US government to force Congress to fund his wall. However, as this promise was made at a rally, it can be categorised as even less binding than his usual undertakings.

Shortcomings

Border walls have been proven to be an effective method of preventing illegal immigrants from entering the United States via its southern border unless those people employ such methods as:

- climbing the wall,
- using wirecutters to remove the barbed wire and climbing over,
- cutting a hole in the wall,
- digging under the wall,
- travelling by boat around the wall, or
- paying people on the US side to help them with any of the above.

A wall along the southern US border would also divide no fewer than three indigenous nations' tribal lands and interrupt wildlife movements, encouraging inbreeding. But all these objections are trivial compared with the president's urgent need to deliver on his promise to build a big, beautiful, expensive, ineffective, environmentally destructive wall.

 Donald J. Trump @realDonaldTrump

My new Plan is that neither Mexico nor America will pay for the Wall. Like any Trump project, we just won't pay the Contractors!

Kanye West and Kim Kardashian West

Kanye 'Yeezy' West is a rapper, music producer, internet philosopher, future political candidate and unlikely Donald Trump supporter. **Kim**

Kardashian West is the most famous of the Kardashian reality television dynasty, and extremely patient with her husband.

Kanye bromance with Trump

Kanye had visited Trump during the transition, to the bemusement of many, and in 2018, he ended his self-imposed Twitter hiatus with a volley of tweets supporting the president, whom he called 'My brother', saying 'We are both dragon energy'. He also posted a photo of himself in a Make America Great Again hat.

Interspersed with the tweets about Trump were observations such as, 'I like ping pong', and a promise to write a philosophy book on Twitter.

Kanye later tweeted that his wife had told him to clarify that he didn't agree with everything Trump had done, and that he doesn't 100 per cent agree with anyone except himself. Those concerned about Kanye's wellbeing were not reassured.

Trump responded, 'Thank you Kanye, very cool!', but did not clarify whether he is indeed dragon energy or West's brother. He has since boasted at a rally about Kanye's support, evidently delighted to have the support of at least one other famous African-American than Omarosa, who had left the White House.

Kim Kardashian West meeting

Kim Kardashian West subsequently met with President Trump about a potential pardon for a drug offender in May 2018, because the guy from *The Apprentice* would obviously consult a Kardashian on justice policy.

Two reality television stars in the Oval Office. The one on the left is far more serious about criminal justice reform. *(US Goverment)*

Kardashian West initiated the meeting after she read on Twitter about a potentially unfair situation, and decided to use her 'influencer' status for good. The woman in question, Alice Marie Johnson, was given a life sentence without parole for a first-time, non-violent drug offence and has now spent two decades in prison. In the Trump administration, famous people tweeting is often the only way to successfully petition the White House, and Trump subsequently commuted Johnson's sentence even though she hadn't appeared on *The Apprentice* and wasn't a political crony. (*See* **Pardon Power**.)

Judicial activists are now planning to reroute all future pleas for clemency via the cast of *Keeping Up With The Kardashians*.

Witch hunt

A **witch hunt** is any unfair pursuit of people that involves moral panic leading to mass hysteria. The term derived from the practice of witch-hunting that occurred in Europe and North America from about 1450 to 1750—the Salem witch trials are a particularly well-known example of the phenomenon, which is now considered both absurd and unjust.

However, the term may also be used to describe a situation where all seventeen US intelligence agencies have agreed conclusively that a foreign power has interfered in an American election, and the Federal Bureau of Investigation, and/or a special counsel appointed by the Department of Justice, is undertaking an independent investigation.

The term 'witch hunt' is especially applicable if any such investigators have the audacity to attempt to discover whether the political campaign that benefited from the interference colluded in any way with that foreign power.

A special prosecutor strings up another round of political staffers.

Instead, the denials of the assisted politician should simply be believed whenever they are issued via Twitter, no matter how many associates and campaign staffers have already pleaded guilty to charges laid as a result of the investigation.

However, a high number of guilty pleas in a particular investigation might make the words 'witch hunt' seem inapplicable, as the common factor in all historical witch hunts is that they never found any witches.

WWE

World Wrestling Entertainment is a sport in much the same way that Fox News is a news channel: there is a superficial stylistic resemblance, but it's actually pure fabrication.

The sport was formerly known as the World Wrestling Federation until the World Wildlife Fund objected, on the grounds of acronym confusion and the exploitation of dumb animals.

Donald J. Trump is the only commander-in-chief to have been inducted into the WWE Hall of Fame, at least until The Rock runs for president. He is also the only president to body-slam a man whose head has been replaced by a CNN logo.

Trump's involvement with the 'sport'

Trump first began working with the WWE in 1988, hosting *WrestleMania IV* in an attempt to bring crowds to his Trump Plaza casino in Atlantic City. Later in his career, Trump would be actively involved in the wrestling and, subsequently, mania.

Trump is not really choking a cable channel in this picture. Fake news!
(Donald Trump/Twitter)

In 2006, during Trump's war of words with Rosie O'Donnell, the WWE staged a match with wrestlers impersonating them. This was roundly criticised, because of course it was, so naturally the WWE organisers decided to go one better and bring Trump himself into the ring. He fought WWE owner and 'villain' Vince McMahon and rained cash* on the audience.

The following year, McMahon and Trump clashed again in the Battle of the Billionaires. The schtick was that the winner would shave the loser's head on live television. It was at the height of Trump's *Apprentice* fame and the ratings were massive, which was surprising given the lack of suspense—obviously Trump would never agree to lose and have his head shaved, as he considers his remaining follicles his most precious asset.

---

* The cash was provided by the WWE, of course.

Trump's next major interaction with the WWE was considerably less successful, however. In 2009, he appeared on *Monday Night Raw* to announce he was buying the program, which, with the accompanying press release, caused WWE shares to drop 7 per cent. The takeover announcement had just been more theatre, but the episode proved that seasoned equities investors had little respect for Trump's business nous and even the sport's investors were unable to differentiate its trademark made-up storylines from reality.

Legacy in political career

Trump's WWE experience foreshadowed his political career in several respects: his love of playing to huge crowds, his popularity with working-class Americans despite his constant boasts about his wealth, and his total indifference to the truth. It also helped to give him an edge: in politics, his showmanship outmatched debate opponents constrained by at least attempting to appear to know what they were talking about. Most importantly of all, WWE taught Trump that even though a contest is (or appears to be) hard fought, the true aim is to entertain the crowd.

For more on Donald Trump, consult Wikipedia.org, the reputable news outlet of your choice or do what he would do and just make up something.